MW00949449

Dr. Angela M. Croone

Galgaliel Angels and D[a]emons

Lucifer's Reign & Satan's Fall

Genesis 1:1-2

Order this book online at www.trafford.com
or email orders@trafford.com

Most Trafford titles are also available at major online book retailers.

Printed in the United States of America.

ISBN: 978-1-4269-4928-9 (sc)
ISBN: 978-1-4269-4929-6 (hc)
ISBN: 978-1-4269-4930-2 (e)

Library of Congress Control Number: 2010917419

Trafford rev. 04/26/2011

www.trafford.com

North America & international
toll-free: 1 888 232 4444 (USA & Canada)
phone: 250 383 6864 • fax: 812 355 4082

Contents

Abbreviations

AHS	Archaic Homo Sapiens
AD	Anno Domini (Year of the Lord)
BC	Before Christ
BCE	Before Common Era
PEN	Paradoxical Episodes Nucleosynthesis
CM³ CC	cubic centimeter Critical Component Temperature
DNA	deoxyribonucleic acid
GA	billion years (before the present)
KA	thousand years (before the present)
MA	million years (before the present)
mtDNA	mitochondrial DNA
PC	progressive creationism

This book is dedicated to my spiritual parents,

Apostle Helen and Bishop George Saddler,

who both have impacted my life spiritually and taught me the deeper things in Christ

1 Corinthians 2:14

Foreword

This book is scholarly and thorough in its content. Within these pages is a vast wealth of knowledge. It's a balanced thesis of the Reign of Lucifer and Satan's Fall. I commend Dr. Croone for her courage in taking on the highly controversial topics of the GENESIS Gap and the pre-Adamic world. She is bold and intelligent in refuting Charles Darwin's flawed theory of evolution. The seed produces after its kind genetically, not by adapting to its surrounding climate, which Dr. Croone asserts would take thousands and thousands of years.

Dr. Croone takes the reader on an in-depth exploration into the mysteries of our past and present world. The immense resources for this book include history, paleontology, science, physics, climatic change, and accurate theology.

This book will awaken the Body of Christ to the many reasons why we have such an adversary as Satan. He once had the dominion over the earth that God has given to us. He, like Adam, was in Eden, the Garden of God. This book is an invasion of light piercing the darkness and exposing it. Jesus came to expose the hidden works of darkness.

Dr. Angela M. Croone is anointed to open our minds to the deep things of God. She is strategic in her warfare and uses her knowledge to alert us to go into a deeper dimension. Her thorough historical and Biblical research in this book will help make the Body of Christ aware of the global and universal activity of our adversary, Satan.

This book takes the reader on a journey from the first Adam to the second Adam, Jesus, who came to give us life and that life more abundantly. We are reminded to occupy our realm, to rule and reign as kings in this life. The book concludes on a high note: God Himself placed His spirit within us; His image will live on when our mortal bodies die, as our spiritual man will return to God and live forever. IT'S ALL ABOUT HIM!

This book is written at the collegiate level; however, I recommend it to all people regardless of educational background. Have a dictionary close by, and expand your mind as well as your vocabulary. This book is sure to open your mind to the deeper things of God.

Linae Lloyd, senior pastor,
Global Faith Fire and Miracles Ministry

Introduction

The environmental climate in Eastern Africa was advantageous and enabled rapid success amid the pre-Adamites like that of Adam formed from the dust of the ground. They lived during the Paleolithic and Epipaleolithic eras, in which perfect atmospheric conditions prevailed in the regions of Africa, which was not affected by the glaciations period. The pre-Adamites accelerated development of advanced technologies that identified these people as human beings, as the first anatomical, genetic modern man. The weather was not only conducive to human life but to the prosperity of plant and animal life as well. It was paradise, with Lucifer, the Angels, and the pre-Adamites all living in unity (super[natural]).

The pre-Adamites were neither apes nor descended from apes. The hominids, who were primitive and apes, could not advance in the things intended for man but could only emulate human behavior. The hominids remained primitive until their extinction in 12 KA; BC. Paleontologists and archeologists describe the advent of modern man as a split occurring in the hominid species, in which one half of the species became human (pre-Adamites) and the other half apes, which is absurd.

The demographical and geological characteristics were ideal for human and animal life; the land was rich and fertile, easy to cultivate. The pre-Adamites resembled Adam, whom GOD had placed in the Garden of Eden. GOD'S PROVISION[S] for humanity was well in hand; the land was fruitful and plentiful in all resources:

ECCLESIASTES 3:11
HE HATH MADE EVERY THING BEAUTIFUL IN HIS TIME: ALSO HE HATH SET THE WORLD IN THEIR HEART, SO THAT NO MAN CAN FIND OUT THE WORK THAT GOD MAKETH FROM THE BEGINNING TO THE END

The oxygen isotope levels in Africa also supported the pre-Adamites; their cognitive behavior, intelligence, and mental facilities were above those of the humans who live today, for they had more usage of their brain before the shift in oxygen isotope levels and the vapor canopy (see page 91), which protected the earth from radiation. The pre-Adamites lived long and prosperous lives; life expectancy for them was more than several hundred years, as it was for other indigenous life and terrestrials. During the Reign of Lucifer, neither sickness nor disease was found among humans or other life forms. ELOHIM created all the inhabitants to live forever sinless.

It was after the fall of Lucifer, the fallen angels, and the sin of man that we unearthed fossil remains that revealed violence and war between archaic *Homo sapiens* (AHS) and man; for example, unearthed fossil remains revealed spear wounds in hominids, and walls were built high around cities for protection (such as Jericho). Not only was Lucifer trafficking malicious and slanderous lies about ELOHIM, but he was also spreading all types of sickness—diseases and deformities that came upon all life forms that would adhere to his lies. This rebellion was not limited to just the natural realm but also affected the supernatural realm; there would be no more sustainability of life. There was a rebuff of harmony amid the nations, man, and animals, for all flesh had corrupted its way upon the earth. Men were hunting animals (including dinosaurs) for food. Hunter gathering *was* the primary food source; men and women (women became more dominant than men) were no longer equals who shared an even distribution of responsibilities.

Women became more dominant and predominantly the ones adding fuel to the fire, becoming shamans and performing cultic religious ceremonies, rituals, and burials. Dwelling in witchcraft and idolatry, they became the receptacles of Lucifer's schemes.

Men and women became high priests and priestesses, offering sacrifices to idols of Lucifer and the fallen angels who had made replicas of themselves as gods, for not all Angels have the appearances of men! Some angels have man and animal parts, and some cannot even be gazed upon because of their frightful appearances (for example, the four living creatures in Ezekiel 1:1–26).

High levels of radiation have been found in caves from the Upper Paleolithic Era, caused by the ramifications of sin; there were many deaths and an array of diseases notwithstanding leprosy amid pre-Adamites and dismemberments of limbs of the *Homo Neanderthalensis* as a result of radon gas (the ozone layer); however, these diseases did not cause a critical amount of disfiguration amid the radon-222 that can be found throughout the earth's outer layer (the product of the decay of radium-226 and uranium-238 is radon-222); during the Upper Paleolithic Era all caves were contaminated with lead-210. The high amounts within these caves could have been a cumulative factor contributing to the early deaths and dismembering of fingers amid the *Homo neanderthalensis* and the deaths of the pre-Adamites. Thus, the earth became cursed and judgment was implemented because of Lucifer's rebellion.

During the early stages of the earth's creation, these isotopes released v-rays consisting of 47 kilo-electron volts, or 113-kilovolt beams of radiation. When decaying, radium begins generating radon gas, which it converts into lead-210. This may also have contributed to some morphological facial features of the *Homo neanderthalensis*.

Lead-210 is an end-stage element; its precursor is uranium. However, between these two solid states are seven isotopes that are gases. The process of uranium-238 transmuting into lead-210 has a half-life of 4.5 billion years; that is, it takes 4.5 billion years for just one half of uranium-238's atoms to decompose and become lead-210. The Radiation during the early stages of the earth's creation and its immense amounts of its complexities is still dissipating this present today.

Prehistoric life forms found from this era fall under the classification associated with rapid burial, for what is not construed as rapid burial would have naturally decayed over the millions of years, as did all other prehistoric life forms and man. What paleontologists have unearthed is the repercussion of sin.

Everything in the earth had been placed in order for this particular age of Lucifer's. There were five major extinction periods to shift the earth's atmosphere and terrestrial and nonterrestrial inhabitants into order. This progressive creation allowed productivity in the plant and animal kingdoms; however, each extinction period (rapid burial) was designed to assist GOD's creative work and process on the earth.

A spoken word from God created the earth. Time was not a factor; once God spoke it, it was done. Man's scientific (physical cosmology) investigations of the creation are based on the *manifestation* (i.e., the materialization) of the earth, the finished product.

The Second Law of Thermodynamics is that which fastens the universe, whereby, implying at an earlier period in time that the universe was created and put into existence, whereas evolutionists have the universe arriving in disorder and producing life forms that, over an extended period, convolute into order. But this is contradictory to God; God is a God of order[1] and not of confusion (i.e., disorder)![2] Nevertheless, evolutionists hide behind the vastness of loopholes in time; not so with the Second Law of Thermodynamics.

Time is an adversary to order; as time increases, an array of disorder amplifies. Unless there is an energy-exchange mechanism, a device that channels energy into something positive, the accumulation of outer energy will accelerate the process of disorder, therefore invalidating evolution, whereby the Second Law of Thermodynamics *exhibits creation.* Both Cambrian radiation periods (530 MA and 70 MA) were characterized by great acceleration in life forms; in the first, multifaceted life forms were phytoplankton[3] (algae) and Calcimcrobes (microorganisms), and in the second, the diversity of animal life forms (see the chart depicting Lucifer's Reign and Satan's Fall on page 79). This acceleration would ultimately

1 1 Corinthians 14:40.

2 1 Corinthians 14:33.

3 Phytoplankton received their energy through photosynthesis, which converts carbon dioxide into organic compounds.

subside in the KT extinction, 65 MA, which would wipe out all but 30 percent of life on Earth.

Phytoplankton is responsible for the majority, if not all, of the earth's oxygen, and without oxygen, the explosion of life forms that was about to occur would have been impossible. Each Cambrian radiation epoch created life forms at an astronomical rate. The earth would go through multiple volcanic radiation events; there would be bolide impacts. These creative sequences of events had an effect not only on the earth as a whole but also on the developmental processes of dinosaurs (terrestrial and non-terrestrial life forms), resulting in modifications of morphological structure and height.

Job ([אִיּוֹב,] meaning "he returns"), is the oldest book of the Bible. Job lived during the Patriarchal era (preceding Moses), which is demonstrated in his worship and sacrifice unto ELOHIM and his domicile in the land of Uz, southeast of Palestine, bordering Edom. The book of Job was written by Moses as spoken by ELOHIM, and it mentions two prehistoric terrestrials: the behemoth and the leviathan. These two dinosaurs (Behemoth: בהמות[4]; Leviathan לויתן[5]) are long after the Cretaceous-Tertiary Extinction (65.5 MA), in which a significant number of life forms perished, although there would be a recurrence after Lucifer's Deluge. It is plausible that Noah's Ark included such terrestrial creatures.

The Archosauromorpha (Greek for "ruling lizard") and the Ichthyosaurs (Greek for "fish lizard") were upon the earth from 300 MA to 65 MA, a period stretching from the Triassic and Jurassic periods to the end of the Cretaceous period, in which the KT extinction would wipe out 70 percent of the prehistoric giant life forms.

Contrary to some beliefs, the characteristics of the behemoth are unlike those of the elephant or the hippopotamus, or river horse. Instead, the behemoth was similar to creatures of the prehistoric era and has been equated with the Palaeotherium, Anoplotherium, Mastodon, or Mammoth. The behemoth is described by GOD in Job 40:15–33. The leviathan (twisted) is mentioned in scripture five times, whereas the behemoth is mentioned only once. The Leviathan is described as an adversary of GOD and as a creature with several heads; in Psalm 74:14, the depiction is similar to that of the *hydra,*

4 Job 40:15–24 (KJV).

5 Psalm 74:14 (KJV).

which has six heads. The leviathan symbolizes a creature the size of a whale, with the appearance of a dragon or a large, horrid sea creature. It bears some resemblance to the Ichthyosaurs clade.

These changes were compulsory for GOD's vision for the earth and HIS desired result. GOD knew what life forms HE had *created* upon the earth, and from creation, the earth had been set in creative shifts. Nothing could alter the creative process that was taking place, for as it was spoken, so it shall come to pass.

Notwithstanding the preparation of Lucifer's Reign, this transitioning of the earth was being put into alignment and *strategically arranged*. The earth was now ready for Lucifer to take possession from 300 KA to 200 KA.

ELOHIM *Describes Leviathan*
Job 41:1–33

JOB CHAPTER 41 LEVIATHAN		
Job 41:1 CANST THOU DRAW OUT LEVIATHAN WITH AN HOOK? OR HIS TONGUE WITH A CORD WHICH THOU LETTEST DOWN?	.JOB 41:12 I WILL NOT CONCEAL HIS PARTS, NOR HIS POWER, NOR HIS COMELY PROPORTION.	JOB 41:23 THE FLAKES OF HIS FLESH ARE JOINED TOGETHER: THEY ARE FIRM IN THEMSELVES; THEY CANNOT BE MOVED.
Job 41:2 CANST THOU PUT AN HOOK INTO HIS NOSE? OR BORE HIS JAW THROUGH WITH A THORN?	JOB 41:13 WHO CAN DISCOVER THE FACE OF HIS GARMENT? OR WHO CAN COME TO HIM WITH HIS DOUBLE BRIDLE ?	JOB 41:24 HIS HEART IS AS FIRM AS A STONE; YEA, AS HARD AS A PIECE OF THE NETHER MILLSTONE.
JOB 41:3 WILL HE MAKE MANY SUPPLICATIONS UNTO THEE? WILL HE SPEAK SOFT WORDS UNTO THEE?	JOB 41:14 WHO CAN OPEN THE DOORS OF HIS FACE? HIS TEETH ARE TERRIBLE ROUND ABOUT	JOB 41:25 WHEN HE RAISETH UP HIMSELF, THE MIGHTY ARE AFRAID: BY REASON OF BREAKINGS THEY PURIFY THEMSELVES.
JOB 41:4 WILL HE MAKE A COVENANT WITH THEE? WILT THOU TAKE HIM FOR A SERVANT FOR EVER?	JOB 41:15 HIS SCALES ARE HIS PRIDE, SHUT UP TOGETHER AS WITH A CLOSE SEAL.	JOB 41:26 THE SWORD OF HIM THAT LAYETH AT HIM CANNOT HOLD: THE SPEAR, THE DART, NOR THE HABERGEON.
JOB 41:5 WILT THOU PLAY WITH HIM AS WITH A BIRD? OR WILT THOU BIND HIM FOR THY MAIDENS?	JOB 41:16 ONE IS SO NEAR TO ANOTHER, THAT NO AIR CAN COME BETWEEN THEM.	JOB 41:27 HE ESTEEMETH IRON AS STRAW, AND BRASS AS ROTTEN WOOD
JOB 41:6 SHALL THE COMPANIONS MAKE A BANQUET OF HIM? SHALL THEY PART HIM AMONG THE MERCHANTS?	JOB 41:17 THEY ARE JOINED ONE TO ANOTHER, THEY STICK TOGETHER, THAT THEY CANNOT BE SUNDERED.	JOB 41:28 THE ARROW CANNOT MAKE HIM FLEE: SLINGSTONES ARE TURNED WITH HIM INTO STUBBLE
JOB 41:7 CANST THOU FILL HIS SKIN WITH BARBED IRONS? OR HIS HEAD WITH FISH SPEARS?	JOB 41:18 BY HIS NEESINGS A LIGHT DOTH SHINE, AND HIS EYES ARE LIKE THE EYELIDS OF THE MORNING	JOB 41:29 DARTS ARE COUNTED AS STUBBLE: HE LAUGHETH AT THE SHAKING OF A SPEAR.
JOB 41:8 BEHOLD, THE HOPE OF HIM IS IN VAIN: SHALL NOT ONE BE CAST DOWN EVEN AT THE SIGHT OF HIM?	JOB 41:19 OUT OF HIS MOUTH GO BURNING LAMPS, AND SPARKS OF FIRE LEAP OUT.	JOB 41:30 SHARP STONES ARE UNDER HIM: HE SPREADETH SHARP POINTED THINGS UPON THE MIRE.
Job 41:9 BEHOLD, THE HOPE OF HIM IS IN VAIN: SHALL NOT ONE BE CAST DOWN EVEN AT THE SIGHT OF HIM?	JOB 41:20 OUT OF HIS NOSTRILS GOETH SMOKE, AS OUT OF A SEETHING POT OR CALDRON.	JOB 41:31 HE MAKETH THE DEEP TO BOIL LIKE A POT: HE MAKETH THE SEA LIKE A POT OF OINTMENT.
JOB 41:10 NONE IS SO FIERCE THAT DARE STIR HIM UP: WHO THEN IS ABLE TO STAND BEFORE ME	JOB 41:21 HIS BREATH KINDLETH COALS, AND A FLAME GOETH OUT OF HIS MOUTH.	JOB 41:32 HE MAKETH A PATH TO SHINE AFTER HIM; ONE WOULD THINK THE DEEP TO BE HOARY.
JOB 41:11 WHO HATH PREVENTED ME, THAT I SHOULD REPAY HIM? WHATSOEVER IS UNDER THE WHOLE HEAVEN IS MINE	JOB 41:22 N HIS NECK REMAINETH STRENGTH, AND SORROW IS TURNED INTO JOY BEFORE HIM	JOB 41:33 UPON EARTH THERE IS NOT HIS LIKE, WHO IS MADE WITHOUT FEAR

For thus saith the Lord that created the heavens; God Himself that formed the earth and made it; He hath established it, He created it not in vain, He formed it to be inhabited: I am the Lord; and there is none else!

Objection to the Genesis Gap

What is the [Genesis] Gap theory?

The GENESIS Gap is the world before the present time that existed between GENESIS 1:1 and GENESIS 1:2, whereby the world that then was, being overflowed with water, perished.[6] Here we have a clear depiction of what had transpired at the end of GENESIS 1:1, which caused the events in GENESIS 1:2. In GENESIS 1:1, GOD is referred to as plural: TRINITY אלהים.:

In the beginning was the WORD, and the WORD was with GOD, and the WORD was GOD[7]; the same was in the beginning with GOD.[8]

GOD created a beautiful, inhabitable earth. It was fruitful[9] in every sense of the word: there were cities[10] and nations (see below), and there was no violence; animal and man lived amid the Angels, all were in perfect harmony. There was no want, there were no diseases, there was no sickness or death; it was like the days of Adam before sin. There was longevity among all life forms (page 91-92). Lucifer (the anointed cherub) had full reign of the earth till he rebelled.

6 2 Peter 3:6.
7 John 1:1 (KJV).
8 John 1:2 (KJV).
9 Jeremiah 4:26.
10 Jeremiah 4:26.

Isaiah 14:12	Jeremiah 4:26	Ezekiel 20:14
How art thou fallen from heaven, O Lucifer, son of the morning! how art thou cut down to the ground, which didst weaken the nations!	I beheld, and, lo, the fruitful place was a wilderness, and all the cities thereof were broken down at the presence of the Lord, and by his fierce anger.	Thou art the anointed cherub that covereth; and I have set thee so: thou wast upon the holy mountain of God; thou hast walked up and down in the midst of the stones of fire.

Genesis 1:2 illustrates utter chaos—an earth that was destroyed, overflowing with water and no light—which is contrary to Genesis 1:1, the original creation of the heaven and the earth (i.e., created [ברא] ; *bara*)[11],

Genesis 1:1	Genesis 1:2
In the beginning God created the heaven and the earth.	And the earth was without form, and void; and darkness was upon the face of the deep. And the Spirit of God moved upon the face of the waters.

11 See Genesis Gap page 1

Where did the pre-Adamites come from?

Jesus Christ is the same yesterday and today and forever. (Hebrews 13:8)

Pedantically speaking, the pre-Adamites were created not unlike Adam, but also fashioned from the dust of the ground. The earth brought forth living creatures (even hominids) of its kind and brought forth foliage after its kind, as that of the waters that brought forth their living creatures. The Cambrian Explosion (sudden life forms) exhibits the six-day (twenty-four-hour days; see page 95) account in GENESIS, which was a recreation of the former earth (GENESIS 1:3–31). GOD gave an anointed cherub dominion over the entire earth (page 13, 71, 79) and all that was in it, with GOD being over all.

The pre-Adamites (anatomically modern humans) originated in Africa approximately 200 KA, BC and migrated throughout the world with their cultural and spiritual beliefs. Pre-Adamites were the first civilization. The pre-Adamites would bring civilization to the rest of the world, through artistry, jewelry, sculpting, musical instruments, religion and burial, industrialization, weaponry, agriculture, hunting, micro tools, and building fortified structures for permanent housing (see Jericho, page 65).

Evidence of the pre-Adamites' civilization had been found in Europe for around 40 KA and South Africa around 75 KA. Some hominids (*Homo neanderthalensis, Homo erectus,* and Cro-Magnon) would become accustomed and learn the ways of the pre-Adamites and would dwell amid them.

1 CORINTHIANS 14:33	LEVITICUS 18:23
FOR GOD IS NOT THE AUTHOR OF CONFUSION BUT OF PEACE, AS IN ALL CHURCHES OF THE SAINTS	NEITHER SHALT THOU LIE WITH ANY BEAST TO DEFILE THYSELF THEREWITH, NEITHER SHALL ANY WOMAN STAND BEFORE A BEAST TO LIE DOWN THERETO: IT IS CONFUSION.

There is no evidence concerning hominids converting, neither a split of speciation one-half being hominid and the other half human. GOD is not the GOD of confusion but of peace. HE is specific and absolute in HIS creating. Beast (חיתו) is beast and man is man (אדם)! Notwithstanding, GOD is transparent when it comes to bestiality.[12] There were accounts of hybridization (see page 39) that occurred during the rebellion of Lucifer (see "The Migration" and "Out of Africa," page 53).

12 Whosoever lieth with a beast shall surely be put to death (Exodus 22:19).

Genesis 1:2

AND THE EARTH WAS WITHOUT FORM (תהו, *tohow*), AND VOID (בהו, *bohow*); AND DARKNESS (שחך, *choshek*) WAS UPON THE FACE OF THE DEEP. AND THE SPIRIT (רוח, *ruwach*) OF GOD MOVED UPON THE FACE OF THE WATERS.[13]

some agnostics have quoted GENESIS 1:2 as being a fragmentary work of creation; however, this is also described by theologians as a gap theory between GENESIS 1:1 and GENESIS 1:2, which bears credence of the fall of Satan that caused the once beautiful and formable earth to become a desolated debacle as a result of *finite* judgment in GENESIS 1:2 versus the virtual beginning in GENESIS 1:1.

However, we have an illustration giving by Moses, which categorically states the condition of the earth in its chaotic state; this is not, however, the initial creative condition of the earth. Needless to say, such conditions are not a result or ramification of GOD'S creative work. The earth was *without form* (תהו, *tohuw* [nought, vain, vanity, waste, wilderness]) and *void* (בהו, *bohuw* [*ruin*—emptiness, void]). These two words, *tohuw* and *bohuw*, illustrate a perplexity of chaos. That which was first created, formed, and inhabited now was an (visible) indescribable accumulation of matter inlaid with unidentifiable materials:

13 Genesis 1:2 (KJV).

> For thus saith the Lord that created [*bara*] the heavens; God himself that formed [*yatsar*] the earth and made it; he hath established it, he created it not in vain [[תהו, *tohow*], he formed it to be inhabited: I am the Lord; and there is none else.[14]

As we read in Isaiah 45:18, Elohim created the earth not in *vain* (תהו, *tohuw*). Here again we recognize the same word, tohuw, which clearly shows that the earth was not rendered in its former condition, as mentioned in Genesis 1:2, as we read of the cataclysmic condition of the earth before Elohim re-creating it. Let's go on a little further into Isaiah 45:18, where it says that Elohim established and formed the earth to be inhabited, which is a far cry from what is stated in Genesis 1:2, for the earth was formed and previously inhabited before Genesis 1:2.
This word, תהו(*tohuw*) is often used by the prophet Isaiah (740–700 bc). He would use this word eleven times in scripture, yet the word is documented only nineteen times through the Old Testament; needless to say, Isaiah's use of the word negates anything good.

The prophet Jeremiah (born 648 bc, during the reign of King Josiah 626–609 bc) would prophesy: "I beheld the earth, and, lo, it was without form and void (תהו ובהו , *tohuw va bohuw*); and the heavens, and they had no light."[15] Here we read the same chaotic condition of the earth before Adam describing the same formless version of the earth in Genesis 1:2. Although we have the same Hebrew idiom (תהו ובהו (*tohuw va bohuw*; without form, and void), the prophet Jeremiah depicted the scenario given in Genesis 1:2 as the pending judgment that was going to befall Judah—a judgment like that of the earth in Genesis 1:2, with no stone left unturned and all perishing.

14 Isaiah 45:18 (KJV).

15 Jeremiah 4:23

JEREMIAH 4:23-26

JEREMIAH 4:23	JEREMIAH 4: 25
I BEHELD THE EARTH, AND, LO, IT WAS WITHOUT FORM, AND VOID; AND THE HEAVENS, AND THEY HAD NO LIGHT.	I BEHELD, AND, LO, THERE WAS NO MAN, AND ALL THE BIRDS OF THE HEAVENS WERE FLED.
JEREMIAH 4:24	**JEREMIAH 4:26**
I BEHELD THE MOUNTAINS, AND, LO, THEY TREMBLED, AND ALL THE HILLS MOVED LIGHTLY	I BEHELD, AND, LO, THE FRUITFUL PLACE WAS A WILDERNESS, AND ALL **THE CITIES THEREOF WERE BROKEN DOWN** AT THE PRESENCE OF THE LORD, AND BY HIS FIERCE ANGER.

The prophet JEREMIAH gave a descriptive account of the pre-Adamites' world that was in a calamitous state; this once fruitful place was now absent of men and fowl and had become a wilderness. Cities were broken down at the presence of GOD and by His fierce anger, albeit that verse 23 reiterates the GENESIS 1:2 account: the earth without *form* and *void* (תהו ובהו). Throughout the Word of GOD, there is no other catastrophic event like this event after the deluge of Noah that further depicts the association of both realms supernatural and natural.

IN THE BEGINNING GOD CREATED THE HEAVEN AND THE EARTH.[16]

This Hebrew word (**ברא**, *bara*) means "new or original creation"; bringing the invisible into visible; whereas nothing was preexistent; whereby it could not be said that the things that are seen are not made of the things that appear; like Moses and the Apostle Paul, both sharing that GOD created all out of zero; nil.

16 Genesis 1:1 (KJV).

THROUGH FAITH WE UNDERSTAND
THAT THE WORLDS WERE FRAME BY THE
WORD OF GOD, SO THINGS WHICH
ARE SEEN WERE NOT MADE OF THINGS WHICH DO
APPEAR.[17]

The entire universe and all the planets were fashioned by the spoken command (*rhema*) of the ELOHIM, the power in HIS WORD. The worlds that GOD had created were made visible. The accretion of liquid matter expanded when made visible out of that which did not exist, only by the spoken WORD (***Λογος*** [JESUS, יְהוֹשֻׁעַ, YEHÔSHUA]) of GOD in which all things exist. Nothing exists without Him, for by Him were all things created that are in heaven and that are in earth, visible and invisible.[18] In the beginning was the WORD, and the WORD was with GOD, and the WORD was GOD.[19]

The world is pre-ordained manifestation of the physical realm (i.e., universe), upholding its function and government, solely based on the spoken *Word* (*rhema)* of GOD.

The word *created* appears in the Bible *fifty-four* times. It is used in regard to the original creation of the physical realm (universe; GENESIS 1:1), the non-existing coming into existence. It is used by ELOHIM creating man in HIS own image (GENESIS 1:27), the first time ELOHIM created man and woman in *His own image,* and then again when creating the marine life and the fowl of the air (GENESIS 1:21).

The word *make* [עָשָׂה NA *asah*] appears in the Bible 2,600 times; *made* and *make* imply use of preexisting material, as in the first use, in GENESIS 1:7, when the LORD made the firmament; here the word *made* (*asah*) is used, for the firmament was preexisting; thus absent dominance in *bara.* We also read in GENESIS 1:25 that GOD made the beasts of the earth; here also, confirming animals existed during the Reign of Lucifer (הֵילֵל, Heylel) now being recreated for the dominion of Adam.

17 Hebrews 11:3 (KJV).
18 Col. 1:16 (KJV).
19 John 1:1 (KJV).

Created (*bara*), nonexisting	Make and made (*asah*), preexisting
Genesis 1:1	**Genesis 1:7**
In the beginning God **created** the heaven and the earth.	And God **made** the firmament, and divided the waters which were under the firmament from the waters which were above the firmament: and it was so.
Genesis 1:27	**Genesis 1:25**
So God **created** man in his own image, in the image of God **created** he him; male and female **created** he them.	And God **made** the beast of the earth after his kind, and cattle after their kind, and every thing that creepeth upon the earth after his kind: and God saw that it was good
Genesis 6:7	**Genesis 3:21**
And the Lord said, I will destroy man whom I have **created** from the face of the earth; both man, and beast, and the creeping thing, and the fowls of the air; for it repenteth me that I have made them.	Unto Adam also and to his wife did the Lord God **make** coats of skins, and clothed them
Isaiah 40:26	**Genesis 6:14**
Lift up your eyes on high, and behold who hath **created** these things, that bringeth out their host by number: he calleth them all by names by the greatness of his might, for that he is strong in power; not one faileth.	**Make** thee an ark of gopher wood; rooms shalt thou make in the ark, and shalt pitch it within and without with pitch.

Isaiah 14:12–15

Isaiah 14:12	Isaiah 14:!4
How art thou fallen from heaven, O Lucifer, son of the morning! how art thou cut down to the ground, which didst weaken the nations!	**I will** ascend above the heights of the clouds; **I will** be like the most High.
Isaiah 14:13	**Isaiah 14:15**
For thou hast said in thine heart, **I will** ascend into heaven, **I will** exalt my throne above the stars of God: **I will** sit also upon the mount of the congregation, in the sides of the north:	Yet thou shalt be brought down to hell, to the sides of the pit.

Lucifer means “morning star” (Hebrew הילל, *heilel*). Here we have the notorious, momentous ***I wills*** (Isaiah 14:13) in which Lucifer’s heart becomes filled with pride.

Verse 12 substantiates the nations under Lucifer’s rule, albeit nations (see page 69) before Genesis 1:2, Adam (Genesis 1:26), to Noah’s deluge (Genesis 7:17–23), and to Abraham (Genesis 17:5).

The pre-Adamites were indeed the occupants of the kingdoms and nations subscribed to Lucifer’s totalitarian rule. Another descriptive account is that of Lucifer’s earthly kingdom, whereby he sits upon *his throne*. Lucifer did not only have reign over this newly created earth but was also able to travel to and from other planetary realms, not limited to heaven.[20] There was also a meeting place in the north (verse 13) where all the chief Angels and Lucifer collectively went before the presence of Elohim as He adjudicated.

Angels give their account of their stewardship at the Mount of the Congregation (Hebrews הר מועד, *ar moed,* appointed sign, time, place of solemn assembly [see page 72]) before God. The governmental administrations of the vast universal Angels were

20 Again there was a day when the sons of God came to present themselves before the Lord, and Satan came also among them to present himself before the Lord. And the Lord said unto Satan, From whence comest thou? And Satan answered the Lord, and said, From going to and fro in the earth, and from walking up and down in it (Job 2:1–2 KJV).

distributed amid the whole entire universe ELOHIM created, which He gave Lucifer rule over. This prophetic vision imparted by ELOHIM in His prophet was an account of a world (*social system*) before Adam. Lucifer weakens (Hebrew שַׁלָּח, meaning "discomfort, decay, waste away and decay") the nation, bringing it down low.

Not only was Lucifer prideful but his momentum and degrees of iniquitous -perversions began permeating throughout the earth. Lucifer planned to defeat ELOHIM and usurp authority over all that ELOHIM had created. Anarchism was greatly distributed amid the pre-Adamites by means of Satan's trafficking; his stringencies of rebellion, violence, and lies would ultimately bring apostasy from the true faith and false allegiance amid men. Not only was the universe created but this was also the origination of sin under the reign of Satan, thus proving wickedness before Adam's dominion. When Adam sinned,[21] it opened up a legal pathway to all that was (in the supernatural realm) wicked, strengthening the rebellion of Satan; manifesting his evil in the natural realm.

As we read in GENESIS 3:6 and GENESIS 3:13, it was a demonic supernatural influence that gained access into the natural to tempt Eve, thus proving that a disembodied spirit could not legally operate in, nor take root (possessing a body) unless permitted, whereby sin had to be initiated and received.

21 And Adam was not deceived, but the woman being deceived was in the transgression (1 Timothy 2:14, KJV).

Genesis 3:6	Genesis 3:13
And when the woman saw that the tree was good for food, and that it was pleasant to the eyes, and a tree to be desired to make one wise, she took of the fruit thereof, and did eat, and gave also unto her husband with her; and he did eat.	And the Lord God said unto the woman, What is this that thou hast done? And the woman said, The serpent beguiled me, and I did eat.

In Isaiah 12:14 Lucifer proclaims his insurgence to heaven before engaging (see page 82 for the will of God and Satan); he goes on to affirm that he will exalt his throne above Elohim and the other Angels (stars [Hebrew בכָוֹכּ, *kowk*ab]), worlds [heaven, earth, and universes], and planets). Lucifer wanted to rule all that Elohim had; the Word of God reads, “The earth is the Lord’s, and the fullness thereof; the world, and they that dwell therein.”[22]

Ecclesiastics 1:9	Ecclesiastics 1:14
The thing that hath been, it is that which shall be; and that which is done is that which shall be done: and there is no new thing under the sun.	I have seen all the works that are done under the sun; and, behold, all is vanity and vexation of spirit.

22 Psalm 24:1 (KJV)

Ezekiel 28:11–17

EZEKIEL 28:11

MOREOVER THE WORD OF THE LORD CAME UNTO ME, SAYING,

EZEKIEL 28:12

SON OF MAN, TAKE UP A LAMENTATION UPON THE KING OF TYRUS, AND SAY UNTO HIM, THUS SAITH THE LORD GOD; THOU SEALEST UP THE SUM, FULL OF WISDOM, AND PERFECT IN BEAUTY.

EZEKIEL 28:13

THOU HAST BEEN IN EDEN THE GARDEN OF GOD; EVERY PRECIOUS STONE WAS THY COVERING, THE SARDIUS, TOPAZ, AND THE DIAMOND, THE BERYL, THE ONYX, AND THE JASPER, THE SAPPHIRE, THE EMERALD, AND THE CARBUNCLE, AND GOLD: THE WORKMANSHIP OF THY TABRETS AND OF THY PIPES WAS PREPARED IN THEE IN THE DAY THAT THOU WAST CREATED.

EZEKIEL 28:14

THOU ART THE ANOINTED CHERUB THAT COVERETH; AND I HAVE SET THEE SO: THOU WAST UPON THE HOLY MOUNTAIN OF GOD; THOU HAST WALKED UP AND DOWN IN THE MIDST OF THE STONES OF FIRE.

EZEKIEL **28:15**

THOU WAST PERFECT IN THY WAYS FROM THE DAY THAT THOU WAST CREATED, **TILL INIQUITY WAS FOUND IN THEE.**

EZEKIEL 28:16 EZEKIEL 28:19

BY THE MULTITUDE OF THY MERCHANDISE THEY HAVE FILLED THE MIDST OF THEE WITH VIOLENCE, AND THOU HAST SINNED: THEREFORE **I WILL CAST THEE AS PROFANE OUT OF THE MOUNTAIN OF GOD**: AND **I WILL DESTROY THEE**, O COVERING CHERUB, FROM THE MIDST OF THE STONES OF FIRE.

EZEKIEL 28:17

THINE HEART WAS LIFTED UP BECAUSE OF THY BEAUTY, THOU HAST CORRUPTED THY WISDOM BY REASON OF THY BRIGHTNESS: **I WILL CAST THEE TO THE GROUND, I WILL LAY THEE BEFORE KINGS,** THAT THEY MAY BEHOLD THEE.

EZEKIEL 28:18

THOU HAST DEFILED THY SANCTUARIES BY THE **MULTITUDE OF THINE INIQUITIES, BY THE INIQUITY OF THY TRAFFICK**; THEREFORE WILL I BRING FORTH A FIRE FROM THE MIDST OF THEE, IT SHALL DEVOUR THEE, AND **I WILL BRING THEE TO ASHES UPON THE EARTH** IN **THE SIGHT OF ALL THEM** THAT BEHOLD THEE.

EZEKIEL 28:19

ALL THEY THAT KNOW THEE AMONG THE **PEOPLE** SHALL BE ASTONISHED AT THEE: THOU SHALT BE A TERROR, AND NEVER SHALT THOU BE ANY MORE.

These verses are not only about a mere man but about Lucifer, GOD's anointed cherub; Lucifer was the most beautiful of GOD's creation, who had been in Eden, the Garden of GOD, and the Holy Mountain of GOD. Satan is barred from the Mountain of GOD (i.e., heaven) but sustains provisional admission.[23] These scriptures cannot be about Adam, although Adam was formed and then placed in Eden, the Garden of God[24] and had access; neither Adam nor the king of Tyrus were covered with precious jewels or walked up and down in the midst of the stones of fire.

Lucifer was also above all Elohim's other creative work, he even out ranked Michael, Gabriel, Uriel, Raphael, Zedekiel, Raquel, and so on.

When Adam sinned, he was cast out of Eden, not the Holy Mountain of God, as Lucifer was (verse 16), but the king of Tyrus received a harsh warning of what was to become of him and his kingdom. Satan was also the dark force (principality) behind the prince of Tyre, so much so that he was called Satan. Ezekiel continues to describe Lucifer by depicting the precious ten stones (ten represents completeness) that were his covering.

Lucifer was created sinless and perfect, as Adam was. Lucifer and Adam had full access to Elohim and the Angelic hosts; all were amid each other till iniquity was found in Lucifer (Genesis 3:6); nevertheless Ezekiel chapter 28 depicts the creation of Lucifer (verse 13) and the fall of Lucifer and the consequences of his fall (verse 18). Nothing was in the way of Lucifer but Elohim, who gave him full dominion and reign over the entire universe, earth, nations, and kingdoms to govern from a seated throne (Isaiah 14:13).

Lucifer even had sanctuaries (Ezekiel 28:18) where the pre-Adamites would gather to worship Elohim. These sanctuaries were established throughout the nations and kingdoms. Lucifer was a merchant (Hebrew רְכֻלָּה, *rᵉkullah*) he would roam throughout the celestial and terrestrial. Lucifer was beautiful and charismatic to all those who beheld him; because of this, he was praised for his beauty, and he was able to seduce and sway one-third of the angelic hosts and pre-Adamites. This same alluring beauty would later become terror, causing astonishment amid the people (Ezekiel 28:19).

23 Again there was a day when the sons of God came to present themselves before the Lord, and Satan came also among them to present himself before the Lord (Job 2:1, KJV).

24 And the Lord God planted a garden eastward in Eden; and there he put the man whom he had formed (Genesis 2:8, KJV).

Before Lucifer's insurgency to heaven, he tried to establish world order throughout the earth, trafficking through the cosmos and building his empire while attempting to overthrow Elohim with his blaspheming, lies, and defiling of the sanctuaries where idols were exhibited while he implemented his audacious treason attempt. Archeologists and paleontologists, who found shrines and false idols buried among the dead, had unearthed evidence of widespread idol worship. This ritual was also found to be a mimic practice amid the archaic *Homo sapiens* (AHS) (apes), representing further iniquities of trafficking. Preventive measures were found in Jericho, where the infamous walls were built; this fortification would be refurbished an estimated fifteen times (see page 65) because of wars. Wars and violence did not occur till after the rebellion of Lucifer; during the earliest stages of Lucifer's reign, there was harmony amid Elohim, men, angels, and beasts.

Nine of the twelve stones (twelve represents government) mentioned in the breastplate of the Aaronic priesthood are the nine stones among the ten that covered Lucifer. The additional three stones on the breastplate of the priest are on the third row of the breastplate; they are Ligure, Agate, and Amethyst.

Elohim's newly ingenious work was completed; the cosmos (universe) was beautiful, as was the earth, in which Eden was the epitome. The Angelic hosts were joyful,[25] worshipping Elohim for his creative work, noteworthy even in his crowning achievement, Lucifer, whom Elohim had created to reign as king (Hebrew מֶלֶךְ, *melek*) over other kings (verse 17) and kingdoms upon the earth; all was beautiful and perfect (i.e., flawless).

There are twelve known Angels of presences that stand before Elohim that can go to and fro before Him. Lucifer is noted amid the twelve. Even after the fall of Satan, he is still allowed to go before God (he is an illegal agent; therefore, permission from God is warranted).

Angels of Presence

Michael	Uriel	Zagzagael	Phanuel
Gabriel	Metatron	Sandalphon	Jehoel
Saraquel	Suriel	Akatriel	Yefefiah

25 When the morning stars sang together, and all the sons of God shouted for joy (Job 38:7, KJV).

Psalm 104:5–9 and 2 Peter 3:5–7

AND **GOD SAID,** LET THE WATERS UNDER THE HEAVEN BE GATHERED TOGETHER UNTO ONE PLACE, AND LET THE DRY LAND APPEAR: AND IT WAS SO.

[10] AND GOD CALLED THE DRY LAND EARTH; AND THE GATHERING TOGETHER OF THE WATERS CALLED HE SEAS: AND GOD SAW THAT IT WAS GOOD.

(GENESIS 1:9–10, KJV)

[5] WHO LAID THE FOUNDATIONS OF THE EARTH, THAT IT SHOULD NOT BE REMOVED FOR EVER.
[6] THOU COVEREDST IT WITH THE DEEP AS WITH A GARMENT: THE WATERS STOOD ABOVE THE MOUNTAINS.
[7] AT THY REBUKE THEY FLED; AT THE VOICE OF THY THUNDER THEY HASTED AWAY.
[8] THEY GO UP BY THE MOUNTAINS; THEY GO DOWN BY THE VALLEYS UNTO THE PLACE WHICH THOU HAST FOUNDED FOR THEM.
[9] THOU HAST SET A BOUND THAT THEY MAY NOT PASS OVER; THAT THEY TURN NOT AGAIN TO COVER THE EARTH.

(PSALM 104:5–9, KJV)

AND **GOD SAID**, LET THERE BE A FIRMAMENT IN THE MIDST OF THE WATERS, AND LET IT DIVIDE THE WATERS FROM THE WATERS.

[7] AND GOD MADE THE FIRMAMENT, AND DIVIDED THE WATERS .WHICH WERE UNDER THE FIRMAMENT FROM THE WATERS WHICH WERE ABOVE THE FIRMAMENT: AND IT WAS SO.

(GENESIS 1:6–7, KJV)

[5] FOR THIS THEY WILLINGLY ARE IGNORANT OF, THAT BY THE WORD OF GOD_THE HEAVENS WERE OF OLD, **AND THE EARTH STANDING OUT OF THE WATER AND IN THE WATER:**
[6] WHEREBY THE WORLD THAT THEN WAS, BEING OVERFLOWED WITH WATER, PERISHED:_
[7] BUT THE HEAVENS AND THE EARTH, WHICH ARE NOW, BY THE SAME WORD ARE KEPT IN STORE, **RESERVED UNTO FIRE AGAINST THE DAY OF JUDGMENT AND PERDITION OF UNGODLY MEN.**
(2 PETER 3:5–7, KJV)

Here is a clear descriptive illustration of the flood that covered the earth; ELOHIM, who created the earth, submerged it in water (deluge). Vapors of water that would rise above and stand above the mountains engulfed the earth, with waters forming a *sea curtain*. At ELOHIM's rebuke, the waters fled; it was the *voice of thunde*r (Hebrew *ra`am,* a peal of thunder), a ringing of thunder that provided an *electrical current,* an eventual cause for a partition between dry land and water. The waters go up by the mountains and down by the valleys unto the place ELOHIM had founded for them. ELOHIM would set a bound that they could not pass over. These boundaries were fixed because of solar and astrophysical magnetism, the earth revolving on its own axis; the power of ELOHIM would cause gravitation of the waters to the heart of the earth, gathering assemblages of the waters into rivers and oceans, creating a boundary in which it will not turn again to cover the earth.

The first descriptive account of the flood is that which occurred after the foundation was laid (Psalm 104:5), although 2 PETER 3:3–7 reveals the same chaotic condition of the earth submerged in water all by the WORD OF GOD! Further transliterations of the scriptures reveals the earth standing out of the water in the water (verse 5). Needless to say, the earth was overflowed with water, *perished* (Greek *apollumi*) (verse 6). A transliteration of GENESIS 1:9–10 says that the earth was already submerged in water and ELOHIM gathered it together in one place (verse 9), causing the dry land to appear and calling the dry land earth (verse 10). Also, PETER discloses that he is describing the *world that then was*, thus illustrating a world (Greek *kosmos,* social system) that preceded this present world that integrated a social system followed by the present, the new earth. The earth was created of liquid substance, the earth comprising an accumulation of liquid. It is probable that this fluid was water, given that 70 percent of the earth is water and the remaining is dry land. This would explain the radiation levels that were expelled during the earth's cooling during the Pre-Cambrian, Archean era (see page 19, "Creation of the Universe and Earth") minutes after its entry in the physical realm (i.e., P.E). The earth would begin to take on form while radiation levels were at their peak. In the Hadean Eon 4.6 GA, the liquid, pliable[26] earth mass formed a rocky terrain, yet it maintained an oblate spheroid shape.

GOD spoke and caused a firmament in the mist (Hebrew *tavek*, "between") of the waters, thus using the firmament to divide the waters that were beneath the firmament from the waters that were above the firmament (Hebrew רקיע, *raqiya*, "expanse"; a visible arch of the sky). Here we have a dispelage[27] of water that was vast, the earth created out of water but also now preserved with the use of water by the same WORD OF GOD are kept in store. It took the WORD OF GOD to create the earth and also the WORD OF GOD to curse the earth and bring judgment upon the earth, by which life was destroyed. There is more water than earth, and this water was used to destroy the first inhabitants.

As the world before was kept, so is the present world kept and reserved unto fire against the *Day of Judgment* and perdition (Greek *apoleia,* "ruin" or "loss" [physical, spiritual, or eternal damnation, destruction, death]) of ungodly men (verse 7). By the word of GOD,[28] the waters were created beneath the firmament; the waters were dry

26 Flexible.

27 Dispersal.

28 Genesis1:1.

land (earth) that would emerge up and above the water, albeit held together by water, the earth risen out of the water. By the very *same principle* the earth was created and it was destroyed—the earth with all its inhabitants—by a spoken WORD OF GOD.[29]

The waters that were above caused the deluge, and the waters beneath—the *fountains of the great deep*—were released from the earth below, and the *windows of heaven were open,*[30] although the light was withheld from the earth, so the water could not vaporize and escape the earth but was retained.

In 2 PETER 3:8 it says that there are those who are willingly ignorant (Greek *lanthano*, "lie hid, be hid unawares") by the WORD OF GOD, being that there had been a world before that had a beginning and an end; whereby, this previous world had been destroyed standing out of the water in the water. But these masses are not just ignorant but willingly ignorant (Greek *thelo,* [obsolete]: "choose" or "prefer"). This is relatively contrary when contrasting the two scriptures to 2 TIMOTHY 2:15,[31] which reads, "study and show yourself approved unto GOD, rightly dividing the WORD OF GOD."

---

29 For this they willingly are ignorant of, that by the word of God the heavens were of old, and the earth standing out of the water and in the water (2 Peter 3:5, KJV).

30 Whereby the world that then was, being overflowed with water, perished (2 Peter 3:6, KJV).

31 Study to shew thyself approved unto God, a workman that needeth not to be ashamed, rightly dividing the word of truth (2 Timothy 2:15, KJV).

Creation of the Universe and Earth

Through faith we understand that the worlds were framed by the word of God, so that things that are seen were not made of things that do appear.

The creation (13.7 GA) of the universe was a supernatural event. The supernatural realm coming into the natural realm (manifestation) was a paradoxical episode, the infinite coming into the finite (time) whence before there was no time. That which was invisible was made visible. Before the universe, nothing existed but ELOHIM.

The *paradoxical episode* (P.E[32].) was a primordial, searing, dense core of elements appearing from nowhere, rapidly expanding while cooling. After in which the liquid mass emerged, it expanded continually while vaguely cooling; within minutes of this initial manifestation of the universe, primordial nucleo synthesis (PEN) took place. Within seconds, an organization of a heavier forms of stable isotopes and unstable isotopes took place rather than the normal light isotopes of hydrogen.

STABLE	UNSTABLE (RADIOACTIVE)
DEUTERIUM (H-2 OR D)	TRITIUM (H-3)
HELIUM (HE-3 AND HE-4)	BERYLLIUM (BE-7 AND BE-8)
LITHIUM (LI-6 AND LI-7)	

32 Phrased coined by Dr. Angela Croone

Deuteron[33] formation preserves neutrons; this heavy form of hydrogen (H^2) is the deuteron that is the core of deuterium. The neutron reaction–proton ratio in thermal equilibrium is maintained (thermodynamic); the tempture reduction is less than the neutron-proton matter differential. These fragile reactions become slower than the universe expansion rate, nevertheless causing the neutron-proton ratio to solidify at about 1 to 6, the main reaction by which neutrons change by neutron decay. Devoid of additional reactions to preserve the neutrons within a secure nucleus, the universe would be of pure oxygen.

As the universe expands, it cools down, promoting stable protons, and creating neutrons that are less stable than helium nuclei, having a propensity to create helium–4 in a creative process of deuterium. In addition, when there is an abrupt element formation the structuring of helium-4 slows till the universe cools and forms deuterium.

It was also during the *paradoxical episode nucleosynthesis* (PEN) that the degree of heat was substantial for mean energy per particle to be higher than the binding energy of deuterium; once deuterium was created, it was destroyed. Nevertheless, the universe would become too cold to create any nuclear synthesis; all elements were affixed, and the only change that occured was PEN decay.

The waters created beneath the firmament were dry land (earth) that would emerge up and above the water; seized collectively by water.[34]

This would transpire three times in scripture: during the first creation, with Adam, and then again with Noah[35]; when judgment was finalized, Earth was below the waters.[36] The earth was made out of liquid matter that did not exist but came about only through the spoken Word of Elohim and therefore made visible! The creation

33 Stable isotope of heavy hydrogen.

34 For this they willingly are ignorant of, that by the word of God the heavens were of old, and the earth standing out of the water and in the water (2 Peter 3:5, KJV).

35 To him that stretched out the earth above the waters: for his mercy *endureth* for ever (Psalm 136:6, KJV).

36 Psalm 104:5–9.

of the earth called for substantial amounts of water and energy; repetitively escaping from earth's atmosphere after its new form were helium and hydrogen. It would be during ELOHIM's creating that the water molecules would be released from the earth's gravity because of the earth's decrease in size during creation. Pressurized, heavy concentrations of CO_2[37] caused the earth plane's temperature to dwindle to 230 degrees, notwithstanding the liquid water oceans.

As the earth temperatures begin to stabilize, there was a reduction of most of the CO_2 as it dissolved in ocean water while the convergence of boundaries (see p.) (continental drift) occurred.

The Pre-Cambrian Super Eon was the earliest stage of the earth. The earth took on form during the universal expansion (PEN), and this liquid earth mass become stony as it cooled during the Hadean Eon 4.6 GA; this period is named Hades (Greek interpretation) because of the rocky state of the earth's terrain. (The Hadean Eon is best known as the beginning formation of the earth.) A preponderance of early rock forms still exists today from the Archean Eon, 3.8 GA. Also, about 3.0 GA, the earth's temperature was 1600 CC; however, these rocks suffered the effects of volcanic explosions, notwithstanding the emissions and metamorphisms because of climate conditions over the billions of years. Igneous (fire) rocks are formed by molten materials that have cooled off and thus solidified; these metamorphic conditions also caused crystallizations of igneous rocks and metamorphic minerals that formed layers to partition various types of minerals on the rocks that petrified[38]. Also it is during the Archean Period the oceans began to appear, although this period was not atmosphere conducive for any terrestrial life form. Subsequent to the 200 MA creation, the atmospheric conditions became conducive for life, allowing earth to stabilize for the introduction of life forms.

Scores of these igneous rocks have been converted into sedimentary rocks, in which lithification[39] has occurred; the

---

37 Carbon dioxide.

38 Petrification is the process by which organic materials become stone. Mineral on the rock became petrified.

39 Rock formation.

diagenesis[40] of these conditions are apparent today. Also, these sedimentary rocks have been found in deepwater sediment. Archean means "beginning" (i.e., origin); during the Proterozoic Eon, the earth's temperature was twice as hot as it is today, whereas that of the Archean Eon was three times greater (1600 CC) than today's current weather conditions.

The elevation of these temperatures was caused by the earth's accretion resulting from creation[41]; this was radiogenic heat, heat from the root of the iron core and uranium radionuclides.

The Proterozoic Eon (25 GA–542 MA) was part of the Pre-cambrian Super-Eon, the Proterozoic Eon; its name means "let life begin." There are three divisions within the Proterozoic Eon, the *first* being Palaeo-Proterozoic Era. It was in this era that isotopes like sulfur, iron, and carbon existed on rocks and minerals. From about 1.6 GA to 2.5 GA, a bacterium named cyanobacteria came into existence. Cyanobacteria are the focal element in the marine nitrogen cycle, transporting oxygen and energy through biochemical processes and photosynthesis. Also during this era, other microscopic, single-celled organisms appeared, such as prokaryotes. Creation accelerated with these life forms increasingly; more outsized, complex organisms would follow the simple life forms (P.C.), which would bridge the way for larger and sundry indigenous life forms, ensuring that the creation cycle would continue.

Molecular biomarkers signify strong evidence of widespread photosynthesis during the Paleo-Protozoic Era. Before there was an increase in oxygen, the earth was anaerobic.[42] Any life forms sustained were anaerobic organisms, which require no oxygen to survive but will expire if the atmospheric condition becomes oxygenic.

The second era of the Proterozoic Eon was the Mesoproterozoic Era, occurring 1.6 GA–1.0 GA; its importance is recognized with the creation Rodina (1.1 GA–7.5 MA), the largest landmass during that era. Rodina eventually broke into three smaller landmasses: Proto-Laurasia, Congo Craton, and Proto-Gondwana.

40 Diagenesis is a metamorphism of chemical, biological, or physical change induced by sediment.

41 In the beginning GOD created the heaven and the earth (GENESIS 1:1, KJV).

42 Without oxygen.

Large objects ranging up to 350 miles wide routinely impacted the earth and caused breakups, separating large landmasses during the periods of extinctions; oceans and continental crust existed within 200 million years of Earth's creation. Such huge impacts would cause the oceans to vaporize within months, therefore causing cloud formations from the hot steam and rock vapors. The height of these clouds would decrease over the next 2.5 thousand years, producing rain and causing the oceans to return to their normal depths.

Sexual reproduction occurred during the Stenian Period (the final period during the Proterozoic Era); however, it was about 700 MA when a rapid increase of terrestrial life forms broke forth after the atmospheric conditions cooled considerably. Sexual reproduction was predominantly limited to microscopic[43] organisms, such as prokaryotes and eukaryotes. Eukaryotes' cells are surrounded by an intricate composition within the membrane-enclosed organelle.[44] In addition, a eukaryote's nucleus is walled in a nuclear envelope, and each of its cells includes an endomembrane system. This finding is based upon the fossils dated back to the Stenian Period (1.2 GA -1GA) from sexually reproducing organisms. Fossil with more composites of eukaryotic cells that are found in terrestrial animals and plants have been found in rocks dating back to1.4 MA.

The third era of the Proterozoic Eon was the Neoproterozoic Era (635 MA–542 MA). It was before the Cambrian Explosion and positioned the Cambrian Era. The Cryogenian Period (from the Greek *Cryos,* "cold," and *GENESIS,* "birth"), beginning 850 MA, was the umbrella epoch of the Neoproterozoic Era. In this period, early terrestrial life forms appeared, for which we have composite fossils.

Ediacara Biotas (multicellular organisms) were primeval life forms from the Neoproterozoic Ediacaran Era that appeared shortly after the dissolving glaciers from the Sturtian Glaciation (750 MA–700 MA). The Sturtian Glaciation is one of the two cosmic glaciation

43 Physical organisms that are so small as to be invisible to the naked eye.

44 Part of the cell that carries out its own designated purpose, together with its own lipid (energy storage) membrane.

eras, the other being the Marinoan; these periods are alleged to have covered the entire earth, creating what is sometimes called the *snowball earth.*

There is strong debate about the snowball earth theory, however, especially whether it was worldwide or regional. Fossil remains of the Cambrian Explosion of 530 MA revealed a rapid increase of *multifaceted terrestrial animal* life forms (biodiversity), a divergence from the Stenian Period. Essential blueprints discovered within these fossils revealed a deceased diagram that would create the origin of new creatures (terrestrial animals). Also discovered from the Cambrian Explosion were calcimicrobes[45] and phytoplankton, which account for most of the oxygen in the earth's atmosphere and half of the world's photosynthetic activity.[46]

There would be resurgences over millions of years; each time, terrestrial and non-terrestrial life forms increased at accelerated levels after each of the five well-known extinction periods.

It is said that these *life forms appeared from nowhere*, which baffled even Charles Darwin, who could not explain this mystery that held an objection to his *theory of evolution* by natural selection. In adaptive selection, each generation adapts to its environment. This is proven by the will to survive and adaptation to its current environment and elements to avoid extinction (extermination); after each extinction, the Lazarus taxon[47] would initiate (name taken from the Word Of God). It did not matter how much a generation tried to survive; bolide impacts were inevitable. Entire taxonomic groups, such as fish, birds, reptiles, mammals, invertebrates, and amphibians, were affected by one or more periods of extinction. Natural selection is based on *heredity traits;* even though morphological changes may occur, a species' DNA[48] factor cannot deviate or evolve into another species, as that of an ape evolving into a anatomically and genetically modern human (pre-Adamite).

---

45 Calcareous colonial microfossils.

46 Using energy from the sun, photosynthesis changes carbon dioxide into organic compounds, mainly sugars.

47 Something that becomes extinct only to reappear later.

48 Deoxyribonucleic acid.

Rapid Burial
The Seven Major and Minor Extinction Periods

A series of catastrophic events before the major catastrophe

These periods of extinction are strategic in the elimination of life forms; this elimination of life forms was not random but an order of specified elimination. There are known to be about seven to fifteen extinctions eras as well as the ultimate extinction that would cause the deluge terminating all life forms that would have occurred before the recreation of the dominion of man (Adam).

These extinction periods provide us with petroleum, natural gases, coal, and other resources for the recreated earth that we know today through vast entombments of terrestrials, vertebrates, invertebrates, aquatic animals, marine mammals, low creatures (insects), and foliage (vegetation) that lived millions and millions of years ago. The most notable of all extinctions is the Permian-Triassic Extinction, which occurred 251 MA, eliminating predominantly *dinosaurs,* aquatic animals (97 percent), and even vegetation.

Around 480 MA, extinction wiped out primarily aquatic life forms, even shellfish (invertebrates). Extinction around 450 MA eliminated predominately marine life (mammals). Several types of terrestrial animals and plants, aquatic and marine life forms, inhabit regions throughout the earth; what may be in one region may not be in another because of climate and environment.

Stratigraphic[49] sequences have occurred over millions and millions of years; scientists have found that some of these rock layers (strata) reveal the different levels of extinctions and catastrophic events leading to fossil remains within the strata. The discovery of these rocks signifies not only death, but also life. The Permian-Triassic Extinction was one of the largest eliminations of foliage (vegetation), and the remains from it created coal. Geographical localities like Oklahoma, Kentucky, Pennsylvania, Indiana, Kansas, West Virginia, and Illinois are prominent coal regions, which means that millions of years ago, these regions had vast amounts of vegetation.

Fossil remains have been discovered deep in the earth at various levels. Between these periods of extinctions, millions of years have passed, allowing a great amount of time for resurgences of life forms to become established and go on for some generations. This acceleration of life forms was caused by radioactivity.

Ordovician Extinctition (480 MA)

This was the first of the series of extinctions ocuring in the Phanerozoic Eon; it was a massive extinction. It is named Cambrian-Ordovician because it happened during the end of the Cambrian and the beginning of the Ordovician Period, in which transition was taking place. This extinction would nearly wipe out the aquatic life forms of shellfish (invertebrates). One of the shellfish species was *Brachipods, a shellfish* that habitates at the bottom of the ocean. Also discovered amid the aquatic fossils from that era were eel-like creatures known as conodots. They became permanently extinct some 20 MA years ago and resembled snails with attenae and a shelled back, which are among 16,500 clades.

49 Rock layers and layering.

ORDOVICIAN–SILURIAN EXTINCTION (450 MA–440 MA)

This extinction was one of the largest, ranking third. The majority of life forms during the Ordovician epoch were aquatic. This extinction period lasted some 10 million years; a large landmass shifted to the South Polar Region, which caused a major atmospheric shift worldwide, causing temperatures to plummet and aquatic levels to become diminutive. This was the second-largest elimination of marine life, the first being of that of the Permian Extinction. Because the climate dropped so dramatically, extinction was immediate, caused by global glaciations throughout the continents; huge amounts of the oceans became sheets of ice.

LATE DEVONIAN EXTINCTION (375 MA-355MA)

This was one of the five great extinctions, in which the terrestrial plants and animals suffered a great loss, though not as massive as the *Agnatha* fishes and their clade, which were almost totally wiped out (the estimated loss was 95 percent). The duration of this extinction occurred in intervals of 3 million years, spanning a total 20 million years. Although this era suffered a great deal of loss, it appears that only the aquatic life forms (plants, low creatures, and fish) were affected, as verified by the fossil remains.

PERMIAN-TRIASSIC EXTINCTION (251 MA)

This extinction period holds prominence above all others based on the eradication, primarily, of all the dinosaurs (Archosaurus), which were the dominant mammals during the Mesozoic Era (251 MA–65 MA). It was the most destructive of all five classes of extinctions periods; the extinction was instantaneous.

The earth has suffered many extinctions, but nothing relative to this one, which occurred at the beginning of the Triassic Period and killed nearly 97 percent of aquatic life forms and 70 percent of terrestrial vertebrates,[50]. Terrestrial vertebrates receive their name based upon their fossil remains, which reveal that they had spinal columns. Fossils that revealed no spinal columns were classified as invertebrates. There are well over 57,000 species within this clade.

50 Bony fish, reptiles, mammals, amphibians, jawless fish, sharks, and birds.

Triassic–Jurassic Extinction (205 MA)

The Phanerozoic Eon major extinction period was the Triassic-Jurassic Extinction, which was an extinction of both terrestrial and non-terrestrial life forms. It is estimated that 20 percent of the marine life forms were exterminated, the majority of them being conodonts (eel-like creatures). About the same percent of land-dwelling life forms was exterminated, primarily the large crurotarsans, clades of the Archosauromorpha. This elimination of life forms ended around 9.5 KA.

Cretaceous-Tertiary Extinction (65.5 MA)

It is alleged that at the end of the Cretaceous Period (65 MA) a temporary extinction that would eliminate immeasurable numbers of life forms in a short period of time was caused by a comet or asteroid measuring 10 kilometers (6.2 miles) wide hit the earth and caused the KT boundary, which caused a decrease of sunlight on the earth of 10 to 20 percent (JEREMIAH 4:23). This extinction wiped out vast amounts of animal life and foliage. Temporarily affecting the earth's environment, it increased oxygen levels to 30–35 percent, causing atmospheric conditions to change with the earth's plane and the first heaven's reprocessing released energies with isolated gases. The release of these gases was induced by the global firestorms that contributed to extensive massive fires, causing global warming.

The vertebrates required 30 million years to recover and make resurgence; and when they did, it was an acceleration of the dinosaurs, primarily the Archosaurus, that dominated these vertebrates and outnumbered other dinosaurs.

Archaic Homo sapiens

Hominidaes (Great Apes)

> The theory of evolution hides behind great expanses of time. Evolutionists' reason, "Given enough time, anything can happen."
>
> —Douglas B. Sharp

Discovered in 1979 in Pakistan, Sivapithecus Indicus (an orangutan), which is alleged to have separated14 MA from the Hominidaes (gorillas and chimps), was the height of a chimpanzee and had the morphological features of an orangutan.

This ape is dated back as early as 12.5 MA –10.5 MA and is described as an *early homo,* a precursor of modern man. Sivapithecus Indicus had large canine teeth and stood five feet tall, and their ancestors were orangutans dated as early as 14 MA.

Over many millions of years, the morphological features and robust stature of hominids have resulted from adapting to their climate conditions, hunting techniques, and hard labor to sustain life, notwithstanding the catastrophic extinction periods and pathological events. According to Wolff's Law if there is a substantial amount of weight bearing down on a specific bone and weight increases, the bone will initially adapt to the weight in a period of time to accommodate it, therefore adapting to the increase by an accumulation of bone mass. The opposite will occur if the bone is not being used; it will become weaker. It is believed that many of the hominids' morphological features have resulted from a host of diseases, such as rickets, microcephaly, syphilis, and rheumatoid arthritis, and from lack of victims. The evidence for this idea is *not conclusive* but explains away their features. Before the fall of Lucifer, however, there was no type of sickness, at least none known to contribute to the change of the whole facial and skeletal appearances of these hominids, neither of which evolved into anatomically and genetically modern humans (pre-Adamites).

It is also known that the hominids' longevity played a key role in their morphological structure, even greater after the fall of Lucifer (three hundred years or more was their life expectancy). These hominids did not morphologically change simultaneously as a collective, because of the various locations and regions in which they dwelt. The maturity (growth) of the hominids was slower than that of modern man. The children of the hominids did not resemble fully matured hominids, whose features would become prognathic during their growth into adulthood; this morphological appearance of the hominids would continue to change, possibly for some three hundred years or more, till death. The cranium would continue to solidify, building additional bone mass. The head and face of the hominids ceased to grow, so the heads became longer and wider as they aged, whereas we see this in gigantism[51] (Nephilim) today.

The hominids had rather poor mechanics (muscle length in the thumb) when it came to handling any type of utensils, let alone painting or carving. They were unable to hold an accurate (precision) grip; like orangutans and chimps, they had to use the last two fingers of their hands to prevent spillage. Their art, mimicking the pre-Adamites, has been unearthed in some caves; it is childlike compared with the more skilled and precise artistry of the_pre-Adamites, which is vivid and very explicit in every detail.

In many cases, paleontologists have unearthed *Homo neanderthalensis* and capped them at forty to forty-five years of age when, in fact, they are nearly three hundred years of age and in most cases, older.

51 Excessive growth of the body or any of its parts, especially as a result of oversecretion of growth hormone by the pituitary gland. Also called *giantism* (Dictionary.com).

The differences in ethnicities has increased throughout the regions of the earth. However, *hardship* is a factor here, and changes have also been caused by environment, diseases, genetics, extinction periods, volcanic activities, radioactive activity, meteoroid (bolide) impacts, and so on. Hominids' genera are gorillas, chimpanzees (pan), and orangutans, proving thus far that apes are apes. These terrestrial life forms have caused much controversy over the years, based on the unearthing of their fossil remains. These primates were predominantly known because of the controversy, which is based upon false truths, thus equating them with Adam.

Throughout the primeval era, amid the cretaceous period, verified was the existence of hominins during that era; paleontologists theorize that the fossil remains date back as far as 7.6 MA –6.0 MA. Paleontologists, biologists, archeologists, and geneticists have unearthed and studied the various subspecies of hominids remains, such as *Australopithecus afarensis*; these remains were diverse in size, form, and strength. Unearthed was the skull of dated back 3.2 MA, the fossil named Lucy,[52] discovered on November 24, 1974, by Johanson and Gray. Lucy was bipedal, had a cranial capacity of 375 to 500 cm^3, was about three feet, eight inches tall, and probably weighed sixty-five pounds when she was alive. Like her predecessor, Ardi, she was described as neither *human nor ape* but as another subspieces of other bipedals. These bipedals' fossil remains resemble those of the pre-Adamites females because of their pelvis and leg bones (bipedal). However, they are still documented as hominids (i.e., apes).

There is quite a debate on these recent discoveries about the bipedal Lucy and Ardi; during their time, there were also chimps and orangutans on the earth that were quadrupedal. Lucy and Ardi bear a resemblance to humans because they were bipedal locomotive, and to apes (which were quadrupedal), but the apes maintained their quadrupedal locomotion, whereas these creatures maintained their bipedal movement. Archeologists, paleontologists, and Darwin presumed to equate this resemblance with evolution to explain the bipedal movement of these primeval creatures as homo, but there were an array of life forms dwelling in the earth in those days. The

52 A gracile australopithecine.

earth was newly created with a variation of life forms that would suffer extinction during the major and minor extinction periods.

Ardi is short for Ardipithecus Ramidus, meaning "ground floor." Ardi was the discovery of Tim White (head researcher) in Ethiopia, 1992–1994. Ardi's cranial size was 300–350 CM^3, one-fifth the size of that of the pre-Adamites at with prognathism unlike that of the pre-Adamites' jaw line. White characterized this fossil under a new genus, the *Ardipthecus*. Unlike Lucy, Ardi could function both bipedally and quadrupedally because of her opposable big toe, which enabled her to climb trees. However, shorter than Lucy, Ardi weighed in at 110 pounds.

The Australopithecus' classification is Mammalia, belonging to the kingdom of Animalia; its clan is Hominidaes. Hominidaes (hominids Great Apes) are substantiated apes (i.e., primates)—first rank; lower rank is hylobatidae otherwise known as gibbon—the primate's clade consists of the following apes: monkeys, tarsiers, and lorisds. Its sub-tribe is Hominidaes. Hominidaes predecessors are Australopithecus Paranthropus, Orrorin, Kenyanthropus, Sahelanthropus, and Ardipithecus. Another sub-tribe is *Hominini*—an anthropomorphic primate (dating back to 4.5 MA –3 MA) that is alleged to be the predecessor of the chimpanzee. Evolutionists not only hypothesize that chimpanzees, humans, and great apes are of the same ancestry (hominids) but also place them in the same classification—hominids—which progressively separated around 4.4 MA, half becoming man and the other half remaining ape, when the whole is ape. But the discovery of Ardi eludes these findings; therefore, these hominids would continue to decrease through the years, crossbreeding with other hominids. *Homo floresiensis*, another subspecies of Hominins, is dated back to 18,000 KA. It remains where it was discovered in 2003, in the Liang Bua cave in Indonesia. Archeologists were able to piece together a skeleton, minus the arms. This particular *Homo floresiensis* stood at four feet, and its brain size (twenty-four cm^3) is smaller than Adam's, whose brain capacity is eighty to ninety cm^3.

> *Here we test the hypothesis that Neanderthalensiss represent a subspecies of H. sapiens by comparing the degree of their morphological differentiation from modern humans to that found within and between 12 species of extant primates. The model taxa comprised 1,000 specimens, including phylogenetic (modern humans and African apes) and ecological (eight papionin taxa) models for Pleistocene humans. Morphological distances between model taxon pairs were compared to the distances between Neanderthalensiss and modern humans obtained by using a randomization technique. Results strongly support a specific distinction for Neanderthalensiss.*
>
> —Morris Craig[53]

53 Neanderthalensis Taxonomy Reconsidered: Implications of 3D Primate Models of Intra- and Interspecific Differences. Communicated by Criag Morris, American Museum of Natural History, New York, NY, December 5, 2003(received February 27, 2003

Adam (1) & Hominidae (Great Ape 2-15) Chart

	MAN	BRAIN SIZE	HEIGHT	DATED	LOCATIONS
1	ADAM / HUMAN (SPIRIT)	1,310-1,475CM3 (80-90IN3)	5'6 - UP	6,000KA/4000BC	GARDEN OF EDEN GLOBAL
2	PRE-ADAMITES HUMAN (SPIRIT)	1,310-1,475CM3 (80-90IN3)	5'6 - UP	300KA-4.5KA	ORIGIN AFRICA
	HOMO SPECIES HOMINIDAE (GREAT APES CHIMPANZEE ORANGUTAN GORILLAS KINGDOM/ CLASS	BRAIN SIZE	HEIGHT	DATED/	LOCATIONS
3	ARCHAIC HOMO SAPIENS (NON-SPIRIT) ANIMALIA / MAMMALIA CHIMPANZEE + HOMO	900-1300 CC		500,000KA	
4	AUSTRALOPITHECUS (APE) "PARANTHROPUS" ANIMALIA / MAMMALIA CHIMPANZEE + HOMO	375-600CC	4'- 4. 5'FT	PLIOCENE 3.9MA-3.0MA	EASTERN AND NORTHERN AFRICA, TANZANIA
5	HOMO ERECTUS ANIMALIA / MAMMALIA	850-980CM3 (60IN3)	5'11IN	EARLY PLEISTOCENE 1.8 MA-1.0MA INDONESIA, ASIA AND EUROPE	AFRICA, ENGLAND, CHINA, VIETNAM, GERMANY, SPAIN
6	HOMO NEANDERTHAL ANIMALIA / MAMMALIA	1,550CC	5.6'FT	PLEISTOCENE 600,000KA	EUROPE, ASIA GERMANY,
7	HOMO FLORESIENSIS (HOBBIT) ANIMALIA / MAMMALIA CHIMPANZEE + HOMO	380CM3 (23IN3)	3.4'-3.7'FT	UPPER PALEOLITHIC 74KA-18KA	INDONESIAN
8	HOMO ERGASTER ANIMALIA / MAMMALIA	700-850CM3	6.1'-6.2'	PLEISTOCENE 1.9MA	TANZANIA, EASTRN AND SOUTHERN AFRICA, ETHIOPIA
9	HOMO HEIDELBERGENSIS ANIMALIA / MAMMALIA CHIMPANZEE + HOMO	1,100-1,350CM3	6FT'	PLEISTOCENE 600KA-400KA GREECE, FRANCE, ARAGO AND ITALY	AFRICA, EUROPE, GERMANY,
10	HOMO HABILIS ANIMALIA / MAMMALIA CHIMPANZEE + HOMO	590-650CC	4'3-4FT	PALEOLITHIC - PLEISTOCENE 2.0MA-1.6MA	AFRICA, TANZANIA, KENYA
11	SAHELANTHROPUS TCHADENSIS (HOPE OF LIFE) ANIMALIA / MAMMALIA CHIMPANZEE + HOMO	340-360CM3		7MA	AFRICA
12	CRO-MAGNON ANIMALIA / MAMMALIA CHIMPANZEE + HOMO	1, 600CC		UPPER PALEOLITHIC 28,000 KA	CENTRAL ASIA, AFRICA EUROPE
13	HOMO GEORGICUS ANIMALIA / MAMMALIA CHIMPANZEE + HOMO	600CM3		PLEISTOCENE 1.8MA	DMANSI GEORGIA
14	HOMO ANTECESSOR ANIMALIA / MAMMALIA CHIMPANZEE + HOMO	1000-1150CM3	5'-6FT'	EARLY PLEISTOCENE 1.2MA-800KA	EUROPE, SPAIN
15	HOMO SAPIENS IDALTU ANIMALIA / MAMMALIA	1450CC3		PLEISTOCENE 195KA	ETHIOPIA
16	HOMO RHODESIENSIS ANIMALIA / MAMMALIA CHIMPANZEE + HOMO	1100ML		PLEISTOCENE 400KA-125KA	SOUTHERN, EASTERN, NORTHERN AFRICA

Homo erectus

Homo erectus (upright man) is dated 1.8 MA –1.3 MA, to the early Pleistocene; *H. Erectus* fossil remains have been found in Africa, Europe, China, Indonesia, and Vietnam. It is alleged that *H. Erectus* derived from *Homo ergaster*, based on their morphological features and cranial size. *Homo erectus* had a large cranial capacity of 850 CM^3 and a height of five feet, eleven inches, up to 30 percent taller than the females (a sign of sexual dimorphism) yet were more robust than archaic *Homo sapiens*. Archaic *Homo sapiens* hunted wild animals for meat, and their diet included fruits and plants, meaning they were omnivorous.

Another subspecies of the *Homo erectus* is *Homo ergaster*. This hominid's domicile was in southern and eastern Africa, about 1.9 MA; fossil remains have been discovered in Tanzania and Ethiopia. *Homo ergaster*'s height was about 6'1 to 6'2',. Another species that is comparative yet in its own classification is *Homo heidelbergensis*, which were more intelligent (cranial capacity 1,100–1,350 CM^3) and robust and the second-tallest among these species, with a height of six feet. There is a 26 percent decrease in the sexual dimorphism of the *Homo erectus*, which produces a slight obtruding facial appearance, a result from prior separation of the species.

Eugene Dubois, an anatomist bent on proving Darwin's theory of evolution, named the *Homo erectus Pithecanthropus erectus*, which means "upright ape-man." When others began to repudiate these findings and referred to the species as upright man, Dubois declined to show his fossil remains of the *Homo erectus*. In 1923 Dubois's refusal to share his fossils would be adjudicated overturning his refusal.

Cro-Magnon

The first fossil remains of this hominid species date back some 35 KA (radiocarbon years) and were found in a Cro-Magnon cave in southwest France, giving the location's name to the species. These fossil remains are described as the earliest European modern man. Louis Lartet, a paleontologist, discovered these five skeletal fossil remains, which were buried with personal items, such as necklaces and pendants, made with animal teeth and primitive tools. Also found in this cave were artifacts like cave paintings, carvings, tools to make wool clothing, and huts made of bones, branches, rocks, clay, and animal hide. The Cro-Magnon lived as recently as 6 KA,BC years ago, simultaneously with the *Homo neanderthalensis*.

Homo-Neanderthalensis

Homo neanderthalensis fossils have been found in Iraq, Israel, Iran, Spain, Greece, and Portugal, with the youngest Neanderthalensis being discovered in the Ukraine. The fossil remains are considered to be from some 30 KA–24 KA. It is documented that Neanderthalensis may have survived as late as 23 KA. They lived during the late Pleistocene Epoch and late glacial age about 1 KA, with the first trait findings discovered from about 650 KA. Neanderthalensis features are allegedly pathological rather than hereditary, given that each ethnicity of *Homo neanderthalensis* has its own separate identity. It has been proven through mitochondrial DNA (MTDNA) that Neanderthalensis are not a strain of pre-Adamites.

The MTDNA of the *Homo neanderthalensis* differs from that of the African pre- Adamites; there is no participation of *Homo neanderthalensis* MTDNA in the pre-Adamites. With this in mind, it is unequivocal that there is no credence to the theory that *Homo neanderthalensis* bear any ancestral responsibility, evolving over the years and converting into pre-Adamites, let alone that they can be characterized as a subspecies documented in 1964. They started as *Homo neanderthalensis* and died out as *Homo neanderthalensis*. *Homo neanderthalensis* is its own separate species!

Homo neanderthalensis was more muscular than Adam. The height of these archaic *Homo sapiens* was five feet, five inches to five foot, six inches (males) and five feet to five feet, two inches (females, a sign of sexual dimorphism). They were built for very cold climates, and their diet consisted exclusively of meats; they were totally bipedal, and their bones were 50 percent thicker than those of

Adam. Neanderthalensis made tools out of antlers and stones, made weapons, such as spears, and knew how to make fires.

Homo neanderthalensis lived in caves and was capable of building housing that lasted about forty-five years. Needless to say, they were able to withstand the climate changes. In their huts, they burrowed out huge holes for poles and bones, with large rocks supporting them to stand against fluctuating climate conditions. For the outer covering of these poles, animal skins (of mammoths) were used, and the animals' internal organs were made into strings to tie the fur onto the poles. Every part of these animals was used, whether it was for food or shelter; nothing went to waste.

It is believed that Neanderthalensis extermination came about through battles with Cro-Magnon; remains have been found of a Neanderthalensis man with a spear wound obtained before his death. It is also alleged, however, that *Homo neanderthalensis* and Cro-Magnon crossbred with each other. Their life spans were relativity shortened because of the environment, the effects of which were amplified by chaotic climate conditions.

Indubitably, archaic *Homo sapiens* dates back more than 6 KA years ago, before Adam. These primeval beings were obtuse and crude and dwelt in caves and huts, having neither intelligence nor technological advances, or living in the fruitful environment of the pre-Adamites. Nevertheless, the time that existed around GENESIS 1:1 and before this scripture provides us with the necessary proof that Archaic *Homo sapiens* lived during the Cambrian Era and that the original creation of the earth goes back some billions of years, proven by rock data and fossil remains that have been dated back to some 700 MA. It was these very life forms that provided us today with such raw materials as fossil fuel (crude oil) and natural gases; there had to be an immense magnitude of flora to live, mature, and die, repeating this sequence many times over to cause an abundance of coal in the parts of the earth where these resources are abundant.

Hybridization

Skhul V

> <u>Allen's rule:</u> The crural and brachial structures (such as limbs) in endotherms (which are prone to heat loss) are reduced in size by means of natural selection in cooler climates. This is a favorable circumstance with the intention to reduce heat loss.[54]
> <u>Bergmann's rule</u>: Geographic races of species possessing smaller body size are found in the warmer parts of the range, and races of larger body size (robusticity of bones) are found in the cooler parts.[55]

It takes thousands of years for body structures to evolve from one to another. Some equate the tropical pre-Adamites of Africa to the Watusis, given their body structures (hyper-tropical); this body structure is typical in tropical countries. If specific pre-Adamites were placed in or exposed to another foreign region, their generations would still exhibit the hyper-tropical body structure if they didn't interbreed. The hyper-tropical body structure differs from the characteristics of the Neanderthalensis, who exhibited short, stocky, robust body structures typical of those who dwell in colder countries (hyper-arctic).

Found in the cave in Mount Carmel, where there appeared to be skeletal remnants of men, women, and children was an incomplete jawbone of a child that is believed to be a hybrid of *Homo neanderthalensis* and modern human, based upon the teeth

54 www.backyardnature.net/ecorules.htm
55 www.backyardnature.net/ecorules.htm

that were unearthed on May 2, 1932, by Theodore McCown *and* Hallum Movius Jr. It was first believed that Skhul V, an adult male hybrid, was a progeny of the *Homo neanderthalensis* because it possessed a brow ridge similar to that of the Neanderthalensis (but there are humans today that bear a resemblance to the brow ridge). It was proven otherwise, however, and was identified as a separate species. Human remains also have been found nearby, at the paleoanthropological site of Qafzeh. The fossil remains at Qafzeh are dated to 100 KA-80KA. The brain case in these remains is of modern human cranial size—1,518 cm^3. There were pre-Adamites already dwelling in the Near East before the *Homo neanderthalensis*, therefore eliminating the validity of the claim that man evolved from *Homo neanderthalensis* or that *Homo neanderthalensis* evolved from pre-Adamites. Although the pre-Adamites would migrate throughout the Middle Eastern world, thereby replacing the archaic *Homo sapiens* (hominids), the emergence would first overtake those archaic *Homo sapiens* in the Levant (Orient) region. Not only did the two-penecontemporary species produced industrial strength they also produce hybrids, whereby evolutionists camouflage their views on this conclusion.

These findings at Qafzeh are considerably different than those in Ethiopia from 1967 to 1974 at the Kibish site near the Omo River: Omo 1 and 2 (hominids). Omo 2 craniophenetically is closer to *Homo neanderthalensis*—primitive; Omo 1 shares morphological with pre-Adamites with archaic features. Other fossil remains were unearthed with Omo 1 and 2: leg bones, four jaws, and partial skulls, and more than two hundred teeth, but very little fauna and few artifacts, which differs from the Mount Carmel cave, which had nearly ten thousand stone tools and fauna. Amid paleo-anthropology the highly controversial topic is the origin of the pre-Adamites.

Before the pre-Adamites, the world was greatly inhabited with archaic *Homo sapiens*, morphologically various assemblages of hominids.

Originating in Africa, pre-Adamites would inhabit the Middle East and Asia; thus, by 40,000 years, they would supersede the hominids, which would become extinct. The pre-Adamites were segregated in Africa till they traveled to the rest of the world, sharing their technology amid the archaic *Homo sapiens*.

Conversely, unimaginatively speaking, *Homo neanderthalensis* was a mere evolutionary epiphenomenonon, an inconsequential and ephemeral adjunction to the archaic account of hominids. Fossil (Lagar Velho child) remains unearthed in Portugal of a four-year-old child suggests that it was a result of hybridization amid *Homo neanderthalensis* and modern human, dated to about 25 KA. Not only a result of hybridization but also generations of the extinct *Homo neanderthalensis*, this assemblage of speciation is found to be arduous to recognize because of the variation of species; hybridization is difficult to exhibit in fossils. This population of hybridization would be characterized as a distinct species; some anthropologists equate such hybrid populations as anomalous[56] forms of the archaic *Homo sapiens*.

The Lagar Velho child (named after the cave) that was unearthed in Portugal with consequential apomorphy of Neanderthalensis traits had affinities to SKHUL V. However, hybridization_does not define the two pieces as one; both pieces are distinct in nature and cannot be equated to the anatomically (genetically) modern humans as distinguished by MTDNA. There is no MTDNA from Neanderthalensis in the pre-Adamite population.

It is speculated that the Lagar Velho child may have been Mosaic rather than a result of hybridization. The Lagar Velho child matured relative to a modern human but yielded Neanderthalensis traits. The teeth reveal that the anterior mandible (jawbone) is larger, which is not that of pre-Adamites. The pre-Adamites are not hybrids but a separate and distinct species and populace. The child exhibited manifestations of modern humans because it did not take on the form of the prognathic face till full maturity, and therefore it resembled pre-Adamites' orthognathic faces, with robust (Neanderthalensis) bodies. However, with this in mind, oversights and exaggerations had to have been substantially high amid unearthing fossils, especially those fossils, which had missing skeletal fragments, craniums, and teeth. The crural (lower leg) index amid the pre-Adamites varied

56 Abnormal.

from eighty-four to eighty-eight (stabilizing at eighty-four for the past 30,000 years) and from seventy-six to eighty-one in hominids.

It would be in the Levant (قرشملا Mashriq)[57] that the *Homo neanderthalensis* and pre-Adamites would encounter each other. The caves of Mount Carmel revealed much of hybridization amid the *Homo neanderthalensis*, whereby the progeny of the two produced hybrids were more advanced than the Neanderthalensis. Some equate this speciation of hybrids being that of Cro-Magnon. Those (Skhul IV and IX) that were found in the caves also revealed the generational hybrids (continuous interbreeding amid the two species); the variation and progression of hybridization, being generational, did not include affinities, having the traits and appearances that still bear that of the Neanderthalensis. Within these caves' burial sites was found red ochre,[58] which was used in burial rituals. Also found in these sites were beads brought out of Africa by anatomically and genetically modern humans (pre-Adamites). Unearthed in levels B and C in the cave of the QAFZEH and in the border of the Mount Carmel cave, amid the Neanderthalensis hybrid fossils in 1933, were found fauna (horses, deer, ox, gazelle, rhinoceros, and hippopotamus), more than a thousand Mousterian tools, biface knives, and two pre-Adamites.

Mugharet Es Skhul (Cave of the Kids), Et Taban (The Oven), Mugharet ej-Jamal (Cave of the Camel), and Kebara all provide evidence of interbreeding of the Neanderthalensis and pre-Adamites; hybrids were found in these four caves. Outside the city of Haifia in Israel is the Cave of the Kids, excavated by Dorothy Garrod, who unearthed the fossil remains of the Natufians, a substantiation of the late Epipalaeolithic era. Amid the remains were scores of microliths and stone tools, with evidence of pre-Adamite burials (100 KA); also found was evidence that *Homo neanderthalensis* resided within the vicinity of the cave approximately 150–40 ka. Amid the caves in Mount Carmel, Mugharet El Wad (Cave of the Valley) was the largest.

57 The geographic link between western Asia, eastern Mediterranean, and northeast Africa.

58 A red pigment that is produced from iron oxide deposits within the earth; unchangeable in color regardless of environment.

MOUNT CARMEL	UNEARTHED
SKHUL I	FOSSIL REMAINS OF INFANT CHILD; AGE 4–4.5 YEARS
SKHUL II	FOSSIL REMAINS OF A FEMALE SKULL AND LONG BONES; AGE 35–40 YEARS
SKHUL III	FOSSIL REMAINS OF AN ADULT MALE, INCLUDING PARTS OF LEFT LEG BONE
SKHUL IV	SKELETAL PARTS OF AN ADULT MALE; AGE 45–50 YEARS
SKHUL V	FOSSILS REMAINS OF A SKULL AND OTHER SKELETAL PARTS OF AN ADULT MALE; AGE 35–40 YEARS

Occupied from 10 KA to 8 KA by the Natufian clan, the cave itself is dated back to 45 KA. These peoples were more advanced in tool manufacturing and cultivation as they transitioned from the Paleolithic to Neolithic; where they had once gathered foliage and hunted game, now they cultivated and raised animals (animal domestication), in large part because of the pre-Adamites. Burials in this location were substantial, given that other caves yielded less. However, this burial ritual revealed a first of its kind sickle blade with a handle carved into the shape of a young animal. Also in burials in this location were found decorative bones and beads, pottery, stone tools, tools to cultivate and harvest grain, microliths, hunting weapons, and stones fashioned for various uses, including as weights for fishing and as blades for skinning animals and scraping hides.

The Natufians were buried in various positions, including the fetal position. The caves in Mount Carmel, along with their fossil remains, have proven to be polemic regarding evolution. The unearthed fossils have been hybrids, which is contrary to Darwin's evolution theories. These caves reveal the relationship of two species as well as speciation. Paleoanthropological tracing indicates that the pre-Adamites and *Homo neanderthalensis* are separate species, thereby affirming the progeny of hybrids.

> *The Skhul/Qafzeh carpometacarpal remains do not have any unique morphologies relative to the other fossil sample remains examined. However, in the functionally significant metacarpal 1 and 3 bases they resemble Upper Paleolithic humans, not Neanderthalensiss. Furthermore, the Skhul/Qafzeh sample differs significantly from the Neanderthalensiss in many other aspects of hand functional anatomy. Given the correlations between changes in tool technologies and functional adaptations seen in the hands of Upper Paleolithic humans, it is concluded that the Skhul/Qafzeh hand remains were adapted to Upper Paleolithic-like manipulative repertoires. These results support the inference of significant behavioral differences between Neanderthalensiss and the Skhul/Qafzeh hominids and indicate that a significant shift in human manipulative behaviors was associated with the earliest stages of the emergence of modern humans.*
>
> —Wesley A. Niewoehner
>
> Behavioral Inferences from the Skhul/Qafzeh Early Modern

It was not till African pre-Adamites migrated out of Africa that their level of astuteness was revealed. The African pre-Adamites had long before exhibited culture maturation before their migration, for they were an intelligent civilization before then.

Unlike the bad angels in GENESIS 6 who taught men much evil (and caused God to repent that he had even created man), here we see clear interpretation of the very opposite: the good angels taught these pre-Adamites before the fall of Lucifer. The African pre-Adamites dwelt amid the angels and worshipped the most high God, ELOHIM.

Homo neanderthalensis were culturally stagnated, unsophisticated for some 65 KA till the pre-Adamites migrated out into Europe, training them and teaching them their customs. This would demonstrate to be effective amid the *Homo Neanderthalensis*, who had no civilities; it was as though they were catapulted forward.

The Neanderthalensis executed some interment rituals and made the same agricultural and hunting tools as the pre-Adamites, as has been substantiated by the findings in the cave of their burial sites.

The pre-Adamite cultural maturation revolutionized the world! It was once believed that Europeans, Asians, Middle Easterners, and others, 75–40 KA, had demonstrated such progression; on the contrary, it was the African pre-Adamite, 200 KA.

Blombos Cave in South Africa yielded much to surprise a substantiation of artifacts that were fashioned by the African pre-Adamites; also found in the cave were sophisticated bone tool, red ochre, decorative coloring and painting (80–75 KA), sixty perforated red ochre (Nassarius) shell beads, awls, figurines, spear points, spatulas, portable art, cave drawings, and multifaceted tool kits. In addition there two stones found in Blombos Cave that also revealed that the pre-Adamites had their own way of communicating and written language based on the intricate geometric carved lines on two stones; these lines represent a set of symbolic language (syntactical language).

> THIS PAST JUNE NOTED THE DISCOVERY OF MIDDLE PALEOLITHIC SHELL BEADS IN COLLECTIONS MADE DURING EXCAVATION OF SITES IN ISRAEL AND ALGERIA MANY DECADES AGO. THE EVIDENCE, COMBINED WITH RECENT FINDS FROM SOUTH AFRICA OF 75,000-YEAR-OLD SHELL BEADS, IS THE EARLIEST INDICATION OF CULTURAL MODERNITY" AMONG ANATOMICALLY MODERN HUMANS—WITH AN ORIGIN IN AFRICA OF ABOUT 200,000 YEARS AGO. BEFORE NOW, THE EARLIEST EVIDENCE FOR CULTURE MODERNITY WAS FROM EUROPE AND DATED TO 40,000 YEARS AGO.

Shell beads were used amid the African pre-Adamites before their migration (200 KA). These shell beads were perforated meticulously (made by a pre-Adamite who has precision grip). The hole in the beads made it possible to make decorative jewelry, spiritual artifacts, ornaments, adornments, and so on. These shell beads (dated back as far as 100 KA) were found in Skhul and Oued Djebbana amid the burial sites, where burial rituals were executed shortly after death. The fossils in SKHUL and Oued Djebbana were of the same genus hybrid (*Homo neanderthalensis* and pre-Adamites) but lived in different places.

SPECIES	LOCATION	LOCATION	NO. BURIED
	MAUDE CAVE	GALILEE, ISRAEL	7
	TSAR 'AIL ROCK SHELTER	LEBANON	3
HYBRID	KRAPINA CAVE	CROATIA	1
HYBRID	VINDIJA CAVE	CROATIA	12
	TABUN CAVE	MOUNT CARMEL, ISRAEL	12
	KRAPINA ROCK SHELTER	CROATIA	77+
	ARCY-SUR-CURE CAVES	FRANCE	26
	GUTTER CAVE	MONTE CIRCA, ITALY	4
HYBRID	STETTEN	GERMANY	1
HYBRID	STAROSEL'S CAVE	UKRAINE	2
	LA FREESIA ROCK SHELTER	FRANCE	8
	KEBARA CAVE	MOUNT CARMEL ISRAEL	21
HYBRID	HAHNOFERSAND	GERMANY	1
HYBRID	EHRINGSDORF	GERMANY	9
	SHANIDAR CAVE	IRAQ	7
	SIMA DE LOS HUESOS	SPAIN	35+
	LA QUINA ROCK SHELTER	FRANCE	25
	ENGIS CAVE	BELGIUM	3
	AMUD CAVE	GALILEE, ISRAEL	16
HYBRID	QAFZEH CAVE	ISRAEL	2
HYBRID	SKHUL CAVE	MOUNT CARMEL, ISRAEL	1

A grand and beautiful design, the earth as conceived by the Creator was an exquisite home for the creatures He had fashioned. The earth itself was a magnificent garden where life flourished in a dazzling display of variety. The ground trembled with the footsteps of the largest creatures (those we now call dinosaurs). Animals filled the trees, the skies and the oceans. From eternity God had planned this creation, and it was perfect in every way. God created men and they began to settle in villages, cities and nations. Angels, a part of this new creation, were given dominion over the earth, to rule with the authority of their Creator. It was the archangel Lucifer who ruled over the nations in all the splendor of the greatest of God's creations. Every creature fashioned by the hand of God acted in perfect obedience to the will of their Creator.

—*Finis Jennings Dake*
Another Time

The Migration

80 KA–60 KA

> *The recognition of Neanderthalensiss as a species distinct from, but sympatric with, early modern humans strongly implies that they were not ancestral to any extant human populations, even if limited interbreeding occurred.*
>
> —*Craig Morris*

Migration of the African pre-Adamites was rapid; it was a sudden dispersal to other territories, including Europe, Asia, and other parts of East Africa. These pre-Adamites appeared like the universe—out of nowhere; GOD spoke it, and it was so! It is a factual hypothesis, based on biblical scripture and conclusive fossil remains, that these pre-Adamites were genetically and anatomically modern humans, advanced in technology. There were archaic *Homo sapiens* that dwelt amid the pre-Adamites in Africa, although the archaic *Homo sapiens* remained in their own nature, having distinct morphological features and structure (frame), and the pre-Adamites remained in their own nature, with continual technological advancement. The pre-Adamites (various cultures) dwelt in homes in cities, whereas the archaic *Homo sapiens* dwelt in caves (troglodytes) and huts.

Homo neanderthalensis fossil remains were found outside of Africa because of their adaptation to cold climates rather than warm climates. This is supported by the cold-adapted animals in the region of the Eastern Mediterranean that dwelt alongside *Homo neanderthalensis*. The pre-Adamites are recognized as dwelling only near the Nile River; Neanderthalensis did not dwell in warm climates. Nonetheless, never separating from the pre-Adamites populace, the Neanderthalensis populace would eventually be over taken by the pre-Adamites, 50–30 KA. There is no evidence of contribution of *Homo neanderthalensis* MTDNA (37 genes) or Y-DNA (78 genes) to modern humans.

When decoding a human being's past, two parts of the human genome are required: the MTDNA and Y chromosome; these two are not involved in the evolutionary process. These two parts of the genome are passed down from generation to generation intact, not part of the evolution process that diversifies in each generation.

Genome blueprints of DNA and MTDNA reveal the disparities between the pre-Adamites and the Neanderthalensiss, which is frequently deduced as opposing the hypothesis that the pre-Adamites and *Homo neanderthalensis* begat hybrids, eschewing the possibility that they are of the same genus.

By tracing the MTDNA (a process known as *lineage analysis*) it has been discovered that the SAN of southern AFRICA, SANDAWE of East Africa, and MBUTI are regenerations of pre-Adamites who have treaded throughout Africa but stayed genetically secluded; it is within these groups that a high quantity of haplogroups are found. These are the pre-Adamites that were the first to disperse. The mitochondria (2) and (3) illustrate a blueprint of biological dispersal from approximately 80 KA to 60 KA.

Descending from (3) were the (M) and (N) macdro haplogroups that became the lineages outside of Africa. The lineages of the (3) were found outside Lucifer of Africa; the group that maintained a low population in Africa was that of (3) (M) and (N).

Under the Reign of Lucifer (300–250 KA), everything and everyone were all of one accord, in unity, albeit synergetic relationship (harmony); there was peace and worshipping of the MOST HIGH GOD, ELOHIM. There was unity among GOD, Lucifer, Angels, men, domesticated animals, and the prehistoric terrestrials. Men built houses and cultivated the land; the pre-Adamites were exceedingly advanced and skillful because of the assistance of the Angels.

Needless to say, during the dispensation of angels, angels taught men how to build their homes, sanctuaries, jewelry, hand tools, hunting weapons, and pottery, etc.

> I beheld, and, lo, there was no man, and
> all the birds of the heavens were fled.
> —Jeremiah 4:25 (KJV)

During the fall of Satan, these pre-Adamites migrated throughout the earth (80 KA –60 KA). The pre-Adamites, while dispersing from Africa, would supplant the archaic *Homo sapiens.* Found amid the fossil remains were hybrids, a mix of the pre-Adamites and archaic *Homo sapiens,* which was and still is forbidden[59]. It is probable that this type of perverseness had occurred after the fall of Satan, along with the enthralling of idols, such as the lion man, Venus fertility goddeses, and god idols, which traveled with the dispersion of the pre-Adamites, for such betrayal, upheaval, or mutiny could have not occurred during the early stages of the Reign of Lucifer, for all were in harmony then. Satan was and is capable of turning men's hearts away from God.

For the iniquity that was found in Lucifer that exalted his pride and led to rebellion and then judgment, those nations that followed Lucifer were placed under a curse, and now all the earth was judged of the iniquitous contagions.

59 Whosoever lieth with a beast shall surely be put to death (Exodus 22:19, KJV).

Out of Africa

Modern Man, the Pre-Adamites

We know now from studies of both the DNA pattern of present–day world populations and surviving skeletal remains that populations that were essentially "modern" in both genetic and an anatomical sense had emerged from Africa by at least 150,000 years ago. We also know that these populations had dispersed from Africa to most parts of the world by at least 40,000 years ago, where they demographically replaced the pre-existing "Archaic populations", such as the European Neanderthalensiss.

—Paul Mellars

The modern man (a.k.a. pre-Adamite) originated from Africa in the Middle Paleolithic Era (80–60 KA) or the Neolithic Era 12–9.5 KA). They had cognitive behavior, human spirit, and intelligence and were socially civilized, which validates their advancement and knowledge in technology and agriculture. With this advancement came an increase in intricacy that created an aggressiveness and assertiveness to compete with other pre-Adamites. There was a rise in the anatomical and genetic pre-Adamites population, even though the Neanderthalensis had decreased due to the extinction (the dansgaard-Oescgern) event occurred during the decrease in isotope levels, in which the *Homo neanderthalensis* could not adapt to climate change. The pre-Adamites had an aggressive lead already, being socially and behaviorally adapted, so they were proficient in obtaining their provisions and resources (hunter gather) The pre-Adamites' cognitive state was endowed with survival techniques; their intelligence and adequacies in technology put them vastly ahead of the hominids (apes; Neanderthalensis), who relied on their animalistic instincts. With both species striving for the same supplies of provisions and resources, one was bound to be eliminated (competitive exclusion). They used controlled fire for cooking, heating, light, and pottery; they built blade tools, projectile weaponry, hand axes, harpoons, rafts, bows and arrows, spears, and spiritual artifacts, and they created music from bones and ivory. Unearthed in a cave in Europe was a flute made from the leg of a bear; the flute had four holes, which on average had two holes. In addition to the flute,[60] other instruments and ivory artifacts were found.

Pre-Adamites also created needles, buttons (that were discovered to have been polished), thread made of animal organs and leather, jewelry, and beads and had access to precious stones. African pre-Adamite technologic advances and social reform would influence the utmost parts of the earth. The Upper Paleolithic revolution dispersed them from 55 KA to 40 KA to Europe and Asia; these African pre-Adamites would then become European pre-Adamites and Asian pre-Adamites. Their technological, congenital behavior became increasingly vibrant over 20 KA. Evidence of such innovation has not been unearthed for the time even before the revolt.

Postulation based on the dissimilarity in ethnicities of the pre-Adamites as distinct species has become known as the polygenism theory. The different ethnicities of the pre-Adamites were created with their dispersal. This theory diverges from that of Darwin, who believed that all pre-Adamites and all ethnicities were of the same species (monogenism) rather than many (polygenism).

Unearthed in southern African caves were more highly skilled weaponry, hunting weapons, and spearheads that also served as tips for arrows. The pre-Adamites had mastered their

60 See page 60.

technology, and their techniques became better, largely because of their environment—*epipaleolithic.*[61]

Leviticus 20:15 (KJV)	Hebrews 13:8 (KJV)
And if a man lie with a beast, he shall surely be put to death: and ye shall slay the beast.	Jesus Christ the same yesterday, and today, and for ever.

These African pre-Adamites were not of the ape ancestry nor evolved (beast and man are separate species). Elohim is not the author of confusion.[62] He is specific and absolute! There was no emergence of the two species till the rebellion of Lucifer, when, polygenists argue, the different races of mankind arose separately in different parts of the world: men went with apes and birthed the Cro-Magnon around 28 ka (it is alleged that the Cro-Magnon are hybrids, of pre-Adamites and hominids). Archeologists describe them as far more intelligent than the former hominids because of their cranial size.

Archeologists and paleontologists regard the sudden appearance of the modern man (*Homo sapiens sapiens*) pre-Adamite as a split within the hominids that produced ape and man (ape is ape). Over the years, the hominids (apes) would mimic the modern-man behaviors, walk upright (bipedal locomotion), hunt, and so on. Because science has no valid explanations where the modern man came from, only bipedal apes, ape, and man are two different species. There are distinctions between them: one is *beast and the other, human*; only sin produced hybrids.

The African pre-Adamites dwelt in Africa from 300 ka to 200 ka. Contributing to their dispersion throughout the world was the fall of Satan. The pre-Adamite had dispersed throughout the Middle East before the fall of Satan, and there was no interbreeding (sin) in Elohim's perfect creation. It was after this that perverseness dawned. God does not condone sin. *Bestiality* is an abomination; there was to be no interbreeding with animals (hominids, great

61 Areas that were not affected by the ice ages.

62 For God is not the author of confusion, but of peace, as in all churches of the saints (1 Corinthians 14:33, KJV).

apes). The African pre-Adamites were created by Elohim (אֱלֹהִים), like the earth, for the *Reign of Lucifer*.

It would be during the rebellion of Lucifer that their creativity in spiritual artifacts would turn false.

At the end of the middle of the Upper Paleolithic Era (100 ka), was the inauguration (but not fulfilled) of judgment[63] being executed, the mountains trembled and the hills moved lightly, and the plate tectonics opened a releasing of radiation, fire, and brimstone from volcanic emissions. During the Upper Paleolithic Era there were caves that were contaminated with lead-210 (Gargas Cave, Tibiran Cave, Maltravieso Cave, and the Mystery Cave). The high amounts of radiation within these caves could have been an accumulative factor contributing to the early deaths and dismembering of limbs amid the *Homo neanderthalensis* and the deaths of the pre-Adamites, whereby the earth became cursed and judgment was implemented because of the rebellion of Lucifer. These pre-Adamites would perish in Lucifer's flood[64] (Neolithic Era) and become disembodied spirits[65] that currently operate in the present-day world as unseen forces.

African pre-Adamites, the *earth's first men,* were not seen until they migrated to the rest of the world at the end of the Middle Paleolithic and into the Upper Paleolithic, placed on earth solely for the Reign of Lucifer; all things must be done in decency and order (point in time).

63 Jeremiah 4:23–27.

64 2 Peter 3:6.

65 Dead things are formed from under the waters, and the inhabitants thereof. Hell is naked before him, and destruction hath no covering (Job 26:5–6; Matthew 12:43).

The Cultures during the Upper Paleolithic

Sauvterrian	Tardendenoisian	Magiemosian	Atiltian	Kbarian	
Starcevo	Virca	Sesko	Choirkoitia	Epigravetian	
Magdalenian	Zagros	Haabinhian	Khandivili	So'nvi	
Pavlovian	Gravettian	Aurignacian	Sangoan	Achheulian	Soanian

During the Upper Paleolithic revolution 40 ka, the pre-Adamites not only revolted to the Middle East, Europe, and Asia but also began crafting artifacts of witchcraft (voodoo figurines), during the rebellion of Lucifer. There was civilization under the Reign of Lucifer; there were also princes and kings[66] within the society, and there was avid worship unto the Creator Elohim (אֱלֹהִים).

As the African pre-Adamites migrated throughout the world, they had greater accessibility to other minerals and undomesticated wildlife to expand; these African pre-Adamites would go on to populate the earth, creating other pre-Adamites ethnicities. Africa's climate was epipaleolithic, for the ice age did not affect them as other parts of the world; they built canoes (seaworthy vessels to travel) that enabled them to travel across the Mediterranean Sea.

These pre-Adamites had fellowship with Angels (angelic influences); needless to say, they were taught these various skills and how to build their cities[67] and kingdoms; proof of this is provided in their artifacts. Many of these artifacts were discovered in Egypt, Ethiopia, and other parts of the earth; these are warm climates (Epipaleolithic areas), which was advantageous to their skill. Reproductions of these forms of angels would become idols (graven images[68]).

66 Thine heart was lifted up because of thy beauty, thou hast corrupted thy wisdom by reason of thy brightness: I will cast thee to the ground, I will lay thee before kings, that they may behold thee (Ezekiel 28:17, KJV).

67 I beheld, and, lo, the fruitful place was a wilderness, and all the cities thereof were broken down at the presence of the Lord, and by his fierce anger (Jeremiah 4:26, KJV).

68 The graven images of their Gods shall ye burn with fire: thou shalt not desire the silver or gold that is on them, nor take it unto thee, lest thou be snared therein: for it is an abomination to the Lord thy God (Deuteronomy 7:25, KJV).

Middle Paleolithic Era and Paleolithic People

Archaic Homo sapiens *and Pre-Adamites*

The archaic *Homo sapiens* are those of ape ancestry (Hominidaes). Homindae had no spirit, for they were apes; animals have no spirits but souls. Archaic *Homo sapiens* had instinct but no intelligence; they could not speak and had no grammatical language as that of pre-Adamites; their form of communication was art and drawing.

The archaic *Homo sapiens* would suffer morphological changes because of climate variations. There were two types of ape species: quadrupedal locomotive and bipedal locomotive. Archaic *Homo sapiens* had skills to mimic other terrestrials. There had been continental shifts, volcanic emissions, and bolide impacts, and these changes all likely contributed to their robust stature and ability to endure these types of fluctuations in environments. These beings would not deviate from their primeval state and animalistic instinct and behaviors. They were rude and obtuse (i.e., beasts). Archaic *Homo sapiens* sustained their stagnation for millions of years, unlike the pre-Adamites. Needless to say, some of the archaic *Homo sapiens* were pets of the pre-Adamites, which would also contribute to their primitive technology by the way of mimicry, not evolution (*monkey see, monkey do*).

The Paleolithic Era was an age of *species* advancement covering achievements in technology (250–200 KA) and the beginning of agriculture of the archaic *Homo sapiens*.

Originating in Africa, modern man[69] Middle Paleolithic 200–150, anatomically[70] a pre-Adamite, was not of ape ancestry but man (the first man), whom God had *created* and formed from the dust of the ground like Adam, but short of the LIKENESS and the IMAGE of the Creator, man's features are *orthognathic*[71] and do not bear the appearance of apes, whereas the chimp, ape, orangutan, and gibbon[72] bear *prognathic* features.[73]

This is the beginning of the *Reign of Lucifer* in the Middle Paleolithic Era. Everything was in order and advantageous to Lucifer's reign; the earth's environment was *rich,* conducive to habitation for all physical life forms terrestrial and non-terrestrial. The land was fruitful, abundant in vegetation and game.

In 1908, Josef Szombathy found in the village of Willendorf, carved of limestone, a female (Venus) statuette dating back to the Aurignacian Period. Pre-Adamites were firing clay to make these spiritual artifacts and pottery (35 KA).

It was during the *Middle Paleolithic* Era (200 KA) that the pre-Adamites believed in a single *Creator* deity and animistic spirits. The pre-Adamites were aware of the supernatural, as evident through their religious belief and artifacts. Inasmuch as they believed in the afterlife, paleontologists have unearthed burial sites that contained religious artifacts; jewelry made with beads and ivory; and clothing made of animal hides, wool, and leather and fastened with bones and antler pins.

Paleontologists have also unearthed stone tools from this era that were often used by the pre-Adamites. In addition to tools, the pre-Adamites also fabricated from these stones hammerheads, spearheads, weapons, *harpoons,* and arrowheads. Pre-Adamites even began constructing rafts, allowing them to be more productive and skillful in their fishing techniques and catapulting harpoons. They used these sea vessels[74] not only to fish but also to inhabit other parts of the planet by crossing the Mediterranean Sea.

69 See page 49

70 Anatomy is the study of the structure of the human body.

71 Straight features.

72 See glossary.

73 Protruding features.

74 The oldest canoe was excavated in Pesse. It dates back to the AURIGNACIAN PERIOD, 82–76 KA.

The Cro-Magnon were known as early modern humans by paleontologists (based on fossil remains), for they were an amalgamation of the pre-Adamites. The last remaining archaic *Homo sapiens* were *Homo floresiensis*, who would ultimately become extinct around 12 KA; the Neolithic Era would belong only to the pre-Adamites.

The pre-Adamites farmed the land and hunted (Middle Paleolithic Era [200 KA]—Neolithic Era 21 BC). The men's hunting weapons of choice were the bow and arrow and the spear, and the women gathered vegetation and kindling. Before this period, the sexual division of physical toil was nonexistent: The women were gender-equal, gaining high status within their society; there was a hierarchal structure within each society. Those women who were within the farming societies (bands) had more pregnancies than those in the hunter-gatherer societies (bands). These hunter-gatherer bands would gather more provisions than they would hunt, gathering 80 percent and hunting only 20 percent. They gathered and procured the meats and vegetation, which proved to be the most effective survival method. They were also skilled fishermen; they barbed fished, trapping catfish as large as six feet long. In the Neolithic Era came pottery, animal husbandry; less hunting and more gathering; domesticated animals, irrigation, wheel agriculture, nations; pharaohs (Egyptian kings), kings, kingdoms, empires, Chinese dynasties, dynasties; villages, towns; and war.

Neolithic Era and Neolithic People

12,000 BC–9500 BC

As the pre-Adamites multiplied throughout the earth, they became more productive at the end of the Paleolithic Era and in the early Neolithic Era (9500–1200 BC), which was the most highly advanced *human* technological era of the pre-Adamites. This would also be the era of the New Stone Age; it was the era of vast farming, in Africa, Asia, and then Europe. It would be the pre-Adamites who would live through the Neolithic Era; the archaic *Homo sapiens* became extinct.

In the Iron Age (*the age of man*, 1200 BC), iron would be melted and forged in Africa. The IRON AGE followed the Stone Age and the Bronze Age; now, farming equipment and weapons were made of iron.

The Bronze Age (Middle East) was the era of adopting the use of metals; it would be the second millenium BC when bronze came into prominent use among men. The Bronze Age came after the Paleolithic and Neolithic in the Middle East, Asia, and Europe. Before the BRONZE AGE, men used stone implements. The BRONZE AGE would usher in the use of metals, when iron would finally be used to fabricate coins and other ornamental things; in 10,000 BC the Bronze Age would come to an end.

The Copper Age (Chaloclithic Era 4300–3300 BC) occurred in the Indus civilization, in southern Turkmenia and northern Iran. This civilization prospered in pottery, which shared similarities with the prior ages, whereby they became quite efficient in making tools hunting weapons, weapons of war, metal tools, wheels, knives, pottery, cooking materials, and much more. Needless to say, the Neolithic era was affluent in agriculture, irrigation, and animal husbandry.

The Neolithic era was the era of communal transformation, with the acceleration of agriculture. Agricultural economics were first established by the Africans who lived north of the equator and cultivated grain (6000-1000 BC). This gave rise to the cities and villages, in which housing became permanent because of the affluence of agriculture. Those regions that had thriving agriculture came to have permanent housing that was made of mud brick reinforced with plaster (with beams that supported the roof). The houses' entryways were built into the roofs, and access into a home was by means of ladders inside and outside of the house. In West Africa, the agricultural force was the kola nut, and African rice during Levant (Mashriq). The first flourishing city was Jericho (9000 BC), with a population of 2,500–3,000.

Jericho 10,500 BC–9500 BC

Cities under the Reign of Lucifer

The world's first municipality, from 10,500–9500 BCE, was Jericho, which housed 2,500–3,000 people and was surrounded by a fortified *stone and marble wall* with a massive tower (23 FEET high) that had an internal staircase. JERICHO was built near the Ein as-Sultan springs. This city was built more than 1,000 FEET below sea level, the lowest city. The original walls were a result of shifts in the earth that caused the region to drop some 2,500 FEET, settling at 1,000 FEET below sea level and causing a inward concave (pit); thus, a fortification wall was established within which the city was built. Dwelling behind these walls were the pre-Adamites, twenty-five cities strong all during the Reign of Lucifer. The original city of Jericho was built 6,000 years before Abraham, and the wall would suffer destruction by Joshua in 1400 BC. Between 6800 BC and 5000 BC something caused the pre-Adamites to abandon Jericho; new inhabitants acquired it and indulged in cultic religion. This is believed to be the onslaught of the rebellion of Lucifer! Afterward, Jericho would suffer many periods of wars and succession by other pre-Adamites, then the Adamites. Soon after the occurrence of this cultic religion, figures of a fertility god and goddess were distributed among local trade; this trafficking would spread like an epidemic throughout the earth. This has been evident through archeological findings from this time period (6800 BC). It is believed that the walls have been reinforced and reconstructed as many as fifteen times.

Before this, reinterating, Lucifer and the Angelic host and men were living in harmony (the supernatural and natural realm). Jericho was described as paradise because of its beauty and natural resources, in which agriculture, economics, and trade were plentiful. Wheat and barley were the primary economical trade, although there has been verification of domestication of animals and hunting. The Jordan River acted as a natural irrigation system with underground streams from the central mountain that replenished the vegetation within the walls. The city possessed a pleasant ambiance, with an abundance of sunlight and a lush oasis of spring waters.

There was not trade only within the walls of Jericho; the inhabitants also traded with other localities (nations). Jericho was the hub of the trading industries; its location was advantageous to their trade negotiations also, being the heaviest traffic of in commercialism. Jericho was an economic hub of trade. The municipality depended on outside resources to sustain itself. Jericho was not only an economic hub but also a religious hub; before the fall of LUCIFER, the inhabitants of Jericho worshipped only the only one and true GOD, ELOHIM.

The NEOLITHIC REVOLUTION enabled other settlers to market within the walls of Jericho as they set up permanent housing on the outside perimeters. This revolution became idyllic bringing stabilization to the settlers and reformation to transhumances and pastoralism. Outside crafts, such as jewelry and pottery, also became highly sophisticated; however, engineering was the husbandry of metalworking.

Another people would spring up some 2,000 years later (7800–5500 BC) in southern Turkey that were more advanced than any other civilization during this era. The town was diversely inhabited, and men and women enjoyed the same social status and therefore sustained equality and power. The population is estimated at 7,700 in a thirty-three-acre location. The town's modest rectangular buildings were tightly adjoined and made of mud bricks; like other Neolithic houses, access was through the rooftops.

The joined houses acted as fortifications for the city, Hunting was inevitable, as was the domestication of animals and farming. Unearthing of this site revealed that agriculture was more lucrative here, not only of grains, as in Jericho, but of peas and berries and agricultural products like berry wine and oil made from vegetables and nuts.

Like in JERICHO, there was evidence of religious shrines, which were built similarly to the houses. The shrines depict a powerful priesthood and sanctuaries, which were elaborate and exhibited the inhabitants' worship. Burial ceremonies were spiritual. Buried among the dead were jewelry, mirrors, and weapons; also unearthed were skulls that were painted, as in JERICHO.

> *Thou hast defiled thy sanctuaries by the multitude of thine iniquities, by the iniquity of thy traffick; therefore will I bring forth a fire from the midst of thee, it shall devour thee, and I will bring thee to ashes upon the earth in the sight of all them that behold thee.*[75]

During the rebellion of Lucifer, a vulgarity of idols and drawings developed, many being sexual in nature, depicting men with large penises in hunting scenes and nude women for fertility. On the walls of theses sanctuaries were paintings of bulls and vultures.

75 Ezekiel 28:18 (KJV).

Kingdoms under Lucifer's Reign

Then	Today	Year
Ain Ghazal	Jordan	7250 BC
Catalhoyuk	Turkey	7500 BC
Cucuteni-Trypillian (2,000 settlements)	Ukraine	5500 BC
Dispilio	Greece	5500 BC
Franchthi	Greece	10,000 BC
Ganj Dareh	Iran	7000 BC
Gobekli Tepe	Turkey	9000 BC
Hemudu	China	5000 BC
Jericho	West Bank	8350 BC
Jhusi	India	7100 BC
Jiahu	China	7000–5800 BC
Knossus	Crete	7000 BC
Lahuradewa	India	9000 BCE
Mehrgarh	Pakistan	7000 BC
Nevali Cori	Turkey	8000 BC
Padah-lin	Myanmar	11,000 BC
Pengtoushan	China	7500 BC
Pentnica	Serbia	6000 BC
Pizzo Di Bodi	Italy	6050 BC
Porodin	Republic of Macedonia	6600 BC
Sammardenchina	Italy	6060 BC
Sesklo	Greece	6850 BC
Spirit Cave	Thailand	9000 BC
Tabon Cave	Palawan	5000 BC

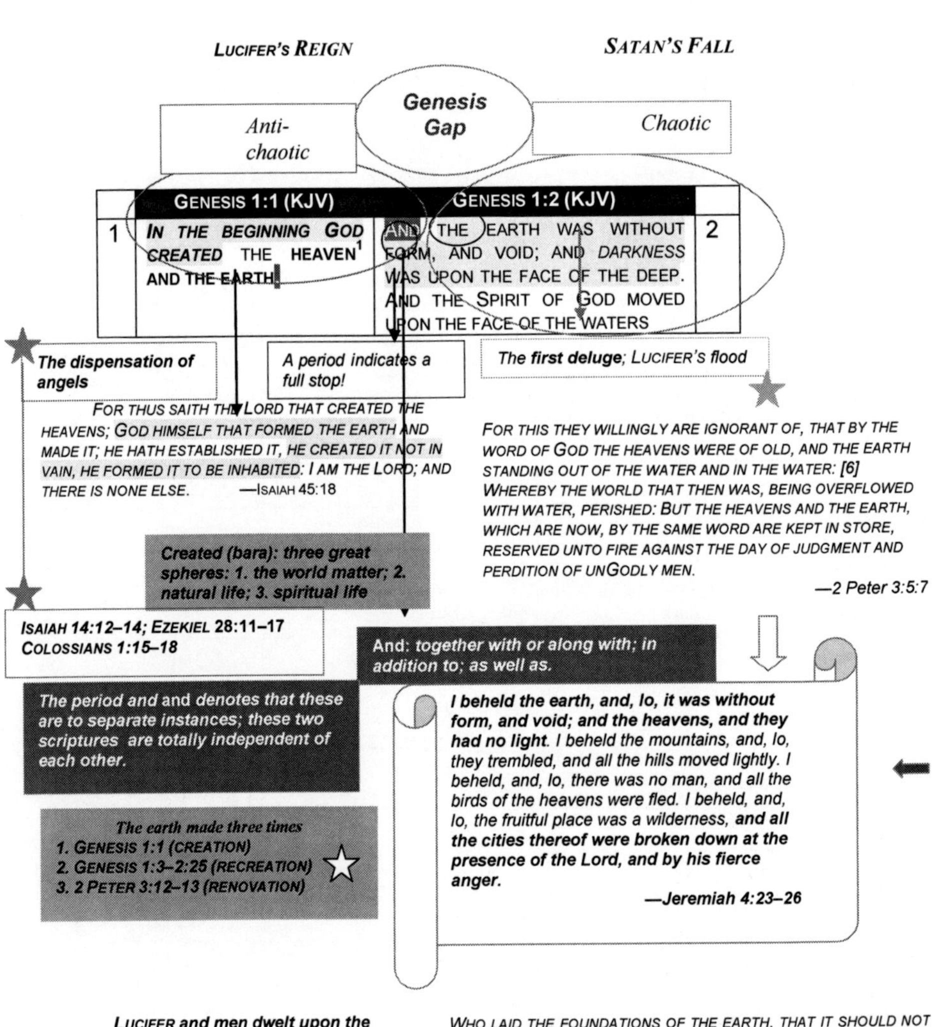

LUCIFER and men dwelt upon the earth prior to his fall (Isaiah 14:14).

WHO LAID THE FOUNDATIONS OF THE EARTH, THAT IT SHOULD NOT BE REMOVED FOR EVER. ***THOU COVEREDST IT WITH THE DEEP AS WITH A GARMENT: THE WATERS STOOD ABOVE THE MOUNTAINS.*** *AT THY REBUKE THEY FLED; AT THE VOICE OF THY THUNDER THEY HASTED AWAY. THEY GO UP BY THE MOUNTAINS; THEY GO DOWN BY THE VALLEYS UNTO THE PLACE WHICH THOU HAST FOUNDED FOR THEM. THOU HAST SET A BOUND THAT THEY MAY NOT PASS OVER; THAT THEY TURN NOT AGAIN TO COVER THE EARTH.* —PSALM 104:5–9 (KJV)

---

[1] Heaven; Hebrew *shamayim,* high places.

Reign of Lucifer

Middle Paleolithic Era–Neolithic Era (200 KA–4 KA)

Thou art the anointed cherub that covereth; and I have set thee so: thou wast upon the holy mountain of GOD; thou hast walked up and down in the midst of the stones of fire.

Ezekiel 20:14

In the beginning GOD created the heaven and the earth,[76] not in vain; HE formed them to be inhabited.[77] Lucifer (הילל[) ruled the earth. The universe was created to complement the earth; the earth and the universe were created simultaneously. Radioactivity was ominous during this creative process,[78] for there was no matter, nothing existed! The universe is vast, with its many PLANETS, SUNS, MOONS, and GALAXIES.

The earth was beautiful and fruitful, with no sickness or diseases, and ready to be wholly inhabited; men were in their full developmental stage; all Lucifer had to do was maintain ELOHIM'S kingdom in the earth. Within this kingdom of heaven is the *governmental office* of the MOST HIGH GOD. It is not stated how long Lucifer's reign was before his fall several hundred thousand years ago as compared with Adam's (אדם)), now 6 KA-PLUS. Under Lucifer's rule, men (pre-Adamites) dwelt in cities[79]; governing

76 Genesis1:1.
77 Isaiah 45:18.
78 Hebrews 11:3.
79 Jeremiah 4:26.

them were princes and kings[80] over nations[81], and Angels. These angels were kings over these nations (*gentile population*)[82] throughout the regions of the earth in which these men dwelt. The earth was and is intended to be the nucleus of the entire world system (universe). During the time of this Dispensation of Angels, all nine angelic hierarchical[83] orders (SERAPHIM, CHERUBIM, THRONES, DOMINION, VIRTUES, POWERS, PRINCIPALITIES, ARCHANGELS, and ANGELS) were all in allegiance with ELOHIM. These Angels were not bound; they are boundless and not restricted to one planetary system or another. They are free to move about throughout the universe[s]. There was an immeasurable host of Angels that were under the totalitarian reign of Lucifer. There were also the pre-Adamites during this Paleolithic Era, created for this epoch and this dispensation. During this dispensation of Angels, there was world order among the Angelic beings. The Mount of the Congregation[84] (הר מועד ; Mount of Assembly) was a place positioned in the north where ELOHIM would present HIMSELF unto HIS chief ANGELS, ANGELS OF PRESENCE, for accountability of the planetary systems they governed.

ANGEL	PLANET	ANGEL	PLANET
RAPHAEL	SUN	MICHAEL	MERCURY
GABRIEL	MOON	URIEL	MARS
BARAKIEL	JUPITER	ANAEL	VENUS
ANACHIEL	SATURN	URIEL	REGENT/SUN

Lucifer had his own throne (ISAIAH 14:13), which established his kingship over the kingdom of heaven and earthly kingdoms; however, Lucifer wanted to be a GOD over all creation and universe

80 Thine heart was lifted up because of thy beauty, thou hast corrupted thy wisdom by reason of thy brightness: I will cast thee to the ground, I will lay thee before kings, that they may behold thee (Ezekiel 28:17).

81 Isaiah 14:12.

82 *Gowy*, rarely (shortened) *goy*, go'-ee; apparently from the same root as Hebrew 1465 (gevah), in the sense of *massing*: a foreign *nation*; hence a *Gentile*; also (figuratively) a *troop* of animals or a *flight* of locusts; Gentile, heathen, nation, people.

83 This hierarchy is larger than nine orders; twelve are known to man.

84 Isaiah 14:13.

and wanted to exalt himself above the chief and prince angels[85] of ELOHIM. He not only had his own throne but also wanted to be seated upon the throne (Merkabah) of the SOVEREIGN *ELOHIM, the throne of the entire universe.*

ELOHIM is Creator of all: the universe, angels, and men; therefore, HIS legitimacy of worship was and is warranted. This also proves that there were kingdoms established not only on earth and heaven but also throughout the universe(s). ELOHIM created the heaven and the earth visible and invisible.[86] GOD is the GOD of the living when He creates it not in vain; there are life forms terrestrial, non-terrestrial (other indigenous life forms), and extraterrestrial.[87]

ELOHIM created Lucifer as the most beautiful and anointed cherub. Even his covering was made of gold and ten precious stones: TOPAZ, SARDIUS, BERYL, DIAMOND, ONYX, JASPER, SAPPHIRE, EMERALD, JASPER, and CARBUNCLE. Lucifer even had tambourines and pipes prepared in him when he was created, for his ministry (mᵉla'kah), even though he was full of wisdom and perfect in beauty. ELOHIM gave Lucifer reign over a newly created earth in which the myriad HOLY ANGELS shouted with joy upon its completion. Everything was plentiful and viable; Lucifer was king over the kingdoms, nations, and cities of the earth, over kings and pre-Adamites.

Lucifer had access to Eden (garden of GOD) and the holy mountain of GOD in which ELOHIM's divine presence rested. Lucifer *was second only to the throne of ELOHIM;* Lucifer was the highest cherub of all angelic beings. Lucifer would join the other angelic chiefs at the Mount of the Congregation,[88] where they would assemble and worship ELOHIM and give accountability of their stewardship.

---

85 Star: *ko-kawb'*; probably from the same as Hebrew 3522 (Kabbown), in the sense of "rolling," or Hebrew 3554 (kavah), in the sense of "blazing: a star (as round or as shining)"; figuratively, a "prince; (stargazer)."

86 Who is the image of the invisible GOD, the firstborn of every creature: For by him were all things created, that are in heaven, and that are in earth, visible and invisible, whether they be thrones, or dominions, or principalities, or powers: all things were created by him, and for him (Colossians 1:15–16, KJV).

87 Extraterrestrial life is defined as life that does not originate on planet earth.

88 And He will summon all the host of the heavens, and all the holy ones above, and the host of GOD, the Cherubic, Seraphin and Ophanim, and all the Angels of power, and all the Angels of principalities (Enoch 61:10).

ELOHIM would call in to account and judge them, seated upon His throne[89] in the north. There is no doubt that there had to be an east, west, and south to the Mount of the Congregation (הר מועד]), but the north seems to be the locality of the throne of GOD (ELOHIM), where the gathering took place. This was not the affixed dwelling place of the SOVEREIGN. He is seated above, He is omnipresent. He rested there as He did on the mercy seat; however, He would meet with the Angelic chief(tan)s. On a synergetic collective, Lucifer and the angelic hosts would all gather and *praise and worship* the MOST HIGH GOD. From here, the angelic chief(tan)s would return to carry out whatever instructions and counsel had been given to them by ELOHIM.

Lucifer was the king of the kingdom of heaven, which was established upon the earth(ly) realm, having great power (dunamis) and authority (exousia) in both the spiritual and natural. Thus he had an influence that was greatly accepted among the terrestrials, Angelic and pre-Adamite (thus, some intelligent being had to teach them survival methods) who had not the spirit of GOD or His ATTRIBUTES or MORALS (image and likeness); these men and animals were *influenced* by Lucifer.

Lucifer was charismatic, beautiful, and full of wisdom. He constructed the building of his kingdom throughout nations, needless to say, orchestrating how things were to be run under his reign. It was during Lucifer's reign that there were dinosaurs, amid other indigenous life forms; apes were apes (with souls), and men were men.

Iniquity was yet to be found in this Angelic being created from fire; his heart still beheld the sacred things of ELOHIM (אֱלֹהִים), his brightness and beauty beheld the luminosity of worship that was pleasing unto ELOHIM. Harmonically played were the tabrets and pipes that had been prepared in him the day he was created. Synergetic in unison, worship would be heard throughout the sanctuaries of the earth where all came together to worship and praise ELOHIM._

Lucifer is more superior than any other angelic being created by ELOHIM thus far, and there will not be any other created like him.

89 For thou hast maintained my right and my cause; thou seatest in the throne judging right (Psalm 9:4, KJV).

Anything that could be given or created unto the utmost highest level of degree by ELOHIM was. Lucifer's love of worship permeated his love for ELOHIM. Lucifer had many assignments, for ANGELS hold many positions and carry out various assignments and responsibilities. Lucifer is a cherub, and cherubim are created to protect and guard; Lucifer was the representation of GOD's holiness.[90]

The WORD OF GOD in EZEKIEL 28:14 describes Lucifer as the anointed cherub that covereth. *Strong's Hebrews* explains "covereth" as *cakak,* meaning to "ENTWINE AS A SCREEN; TO FENCE IN; TO COVER OVER; TO PROTECT; DEFENSE, DEFEND, HEDGE IN, JOIN TOGETHER, SET, SHUT UP." These same things are said of the two GOLDEN CHERUBIM placed on the mercy seat[91] of the Ark of the Covenant, placed in the Tabernacle of the Congregation (אהל מועד), which is the physical (realm) manifestation of the Mountain of the Congregation (הר מועד). Lucifer was one of the two cherubim who guarded the throne of the MOST HIGH GOD.

The Tabernacle of the Congregation was the replica of the Mountain of the Congregation,[92] from which Lucifer had the privilege of going to and fro in the holy mountain of GOD. Later, this would also increase the ammunition of jealousy in the adversary, for man was able to enter into the presence of GOD with worship and praise and man was even placed in EDEN[93] (HEBREW עדן, *ay'-den*), the GARDEN OF GOD, like Lucifer.

Lucifer knew the administration of GOD and how to govern His kingdom; he was wholly gifted, for GOD allowed Lucifer to reign over the earth. Lucifer protected all that which belonged to GOD: Eden (the Garden of GOD), and the Mountain of GOD. In the Kingdom of heaven, he protected all that was sacrosanct to ELOHIM; had the uppermost position that any Angel or man could have. Lucifer is

---

90 Cover, or *sakak*, saw-kak' (Exodus 33:22): a primitive root; properly to *entwine* as a screen; by implication, to *fence* in, *cover* over, (figuratively) *protect*: cover, defense, defend, hedge in, join together, set, shut up.

91 And the cherubim shall stretch forth their wings on high, covering the mercy seat with their wings, and their faces shall look one to another; toward the mercy seat shall the faces of the cherubims be (Exodus 25:20, KJV).

92 See page 78.

93 Thou hast been in Eden the garden of God; every precious stone was thy covering, the sardius, topaz, and the diamond, the beryl, the onyx, and the jasper, the sapphire, the emerald, and the carbuncle, and gold: the workmanship of thy tabrets and of thy pipes was prepared in thee in the day that thou wast created (Ezekiel 28:13, KJV).

also described as being anointed, which means that he was set apart for specific duty.

Lucifer had a free will; he was not bound to the earth and could go anywhere he chose and make his own choices. He would voyage throughout the universe to other planetary systems and to heaven; it is believed that he also dwelt upon the planet Rahab._

Angels like Lucifer are free to journey to remote planetary systems and galaxies in which they are not bound and to cohabit and commune with other Angels. (There is a strong belief that there are *physical life forms* on other planets; however, after researching the sixty-six books of the Bible, I've found nothing to support or dispute those beliefs.) Lucifer had supernatural powers and intelligence and was full of wisdom that enabled him to cultivate and build upon and sustain, to steward, what God had *put into creation*, which involved the pre-Adamites (anatomically and genetically modern humans).

During this Paleolithic Era, these pre-Adamites dwelt in cities and were using *controlled fire* to keep warm and to cook their food. They made weapons (bow and arrows, spears), stone and wood tools, and garments and footgear that were appropriate for the climate (Epipaleolithic).

During the Upper Paleolithic Era, the troglodytes were known for cave art, which was found in caves along with portable art drawn on rocks amid carvings of idols. This was also known as the era of acculturation because the two species (cultures) anatomically and genetically modern humans would come together with Neanderthalensis. The original species would exchange continuously with another, thereby altering the culture of the other to become more industrious. This alteration would manufacture more complex (blade) tools compared with those of the Lower Paleolithic Era—the simple tools (stone tools) that were used among the Acheuleans.

Pre-Adamites practiced spiritual ceremonial rites over their dead while burying them with jewelry and artifacts (necklaces made out of animal bones and ivory and other minerals); they would worship, with their flutes made of bones and ivory and with animal skins serving as drums.

There is no plausible way that the hominids could fabricate such artifacts, because of their thumbs, let alone fabricate such intricate tools (MICROLITHIC) and weapons as those of the pre-Adamites, therefore exhibiting unsophistication, an acquiescence of barbaric weaponry. Hominids' hands were not physically equipped for artistry exhibiting such precise detail; these cave paintings and carvings are not those of hominids but of the pre-Adamites. Still, the Ardipthecus Ramidus fingers were lengthy, with small thumbs and large toes, which enabled climbing and bipedal locomotion.

It is deduced that some Neanderthalensis had some manipulatory capabilities resembling those of the pre-Adamites, yet beyond the scope of the anatomically modern humans (pre-Adamites), who had precision grip.[94] The Neanderthalensis had unusual hypertrophied[95] hand musculature, which disabled them; they where mechanically challenged throughout their hand and (CMC[96]) joints. The Neanderthalensis grip was a power grip,[97] which was obligatory to their genetics, enabling the palm and thumb to serve as a support to hunting and gathering, which required great grip strength.

There is evidence of priests and sanctuary servants during the Paleolithic Era. These sanctuaries[98] were the places where the pre-Adamites worshipped God (and that Satan later defiled). Pre-Adamites were skillful with their hands; a host of their artistry has been found in Lascaux, France, in a cave. The Lascaux cave reveals more than six hundred paintings and slightly more than 140,000 carvings. The paintings illustrate the warm environment during that era; themes illustrate animals like rhinoceros, birds, bison, deer, horses, and aurochs in explicit detail with vivid colors. The paintings also include other illustrations that cannot be decoded.

---

94 Precision grip is made possible by the intermediate phalanges (fingertips) and the thumb pressing against each other. Examples of using precision grip are writing with a pencil, opening a jar with the fingertips alone, and gripping a ball (as long as it is not tight against the palm) (www.wikipedia.org).

95 1. Abnormal enlargement of a part or organ; excessive growth. 2. Excessive growth or accumulation (www.dictionary.com).

96 The basal joint (also known as the carpometacarpal joint or CMC joint) of the thumb is where the metacarpal bone of the thumb attaches to the trapezium bone of the wrist. It is this joint that allows you to move your thumb into your palm—a motion called opposition (www.handuniversity.com).

97 Power grip is formed when the fingers (and sometime palm) clamp down on an object, with the thumb making counter pressure. Examples of using power grip are gripping a hammer, opening a jar using both the palm and fingers, and doing pull-ups (www.wikipedia.org).

98 Ezekiel 28:18.

Mountain (Lucifer) and Tabernacle (Man) of the Congregation

The Mountain of the Congregation and Eden Of God

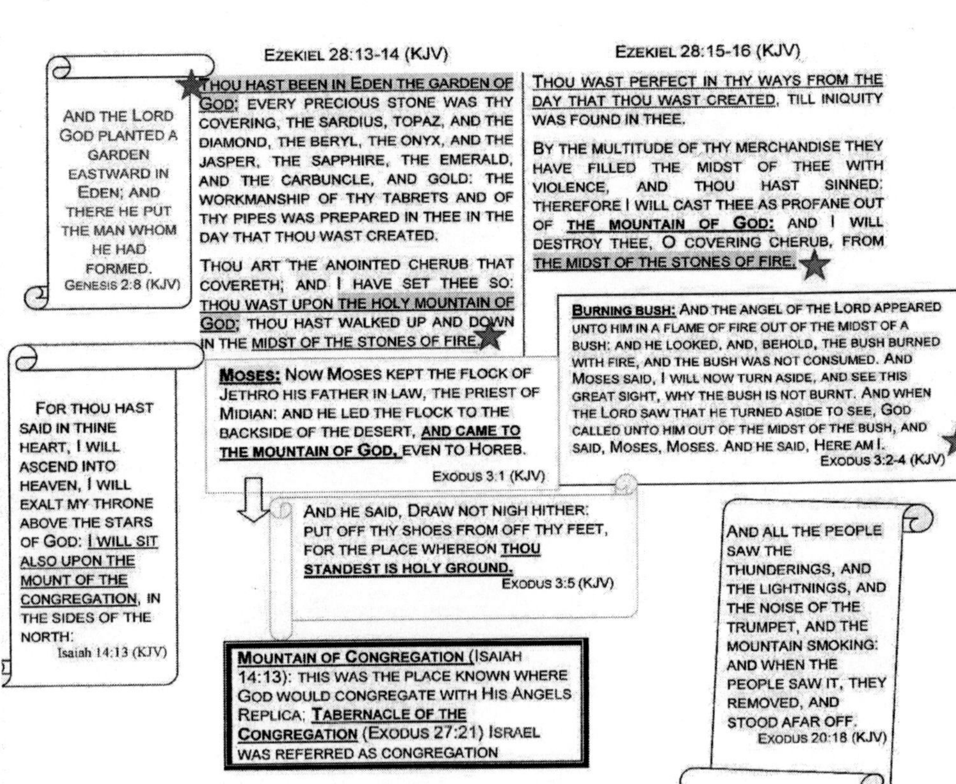

This was the Holy mountain of God, i.e. His secret place

Satan's Fall

Judgment Fulfilled, Neolithic Era (4000 BC)

Adversary LUCIFER *became to* GOD; *therefore name changes to Satan*

It is believed that the number of fallen Angels is substantial; these angels fell for nine days. Scholars in the fifteenth century placed the number at an alarming, astronomical 133,306,668, whereas in other accounts, the number is less, at 7,405,926. Based on scripture, the summative Angels are innumerable; therefore, it is impossible to narrow these hypotheses to higher levels of accuracy, given these high numbers. Angels rule over other planets. Even though these Angels are fallen, they have not lost their ranks, nor did their leader, Lucifer, but he did lose his rule (from king of the former world to prince[99] of the present).

99 Wherein in time past ye walked according to the course of this world, according to the prince of the power of the air, the spirit that now worketh in the children of disobedience (Ephesians 2:2, KJV).

Equated with:	Scriptures	Equated with:	Scriptures
Satan	John 13:27	Father of lies	John 8:44
Tempter	Matthew 4:3	Prince of this world	John 12:31
Power of darkness	Colossians 1:13	Angel of light	2 Corinthians 11:14
Prince of the power of the air	Ephesians 6:12	Adversary	1 Peter 5:8
Abaddon	Revelation 9:11	Angel of the bottomless pit	Revelation 9:11
Son of perdition	John 17:12	Devil	Revelation 20:2
Roaring lion	1 Peter 5:8	Evil spirit	1 Samuel 16:14
Old serpent	Revelation 12:9	God of this world	2 Corinthians 4:4
Belial	2 Corinthians 6:15	Enemy	Matthew 13:39
Dragon	Revelation 12:7	Accuser of the brethren	Revelation 12:10
Apollyon	Revelation 9:11	Antichrist	1 John 4:3

The name Lucifer means "*son of the morning*" and is mentioned in scripture only once. Before his incursion to heaven, Lucifer had weakened the nations in the earth (pre-Adamites). Nevertheless, this defaming of God resulted in violence (Ezekiel 28): God states, "*I will lay thee before kings, that they may behold thee.*"[100] Lucifer's proclamation was that he would ascend to heaven and be like the most high; it ended just as promptly as he had spoken it.

Lucifer traveled throughout the kingdom and nations, spreading slanderous lies defaming God in the multitude of his iniquities, distributing false idols among other traders while steering men's hearts away from God, defiling his own sanctuaries, which became shrines with decorative idols—displays of gods and goddess.

100 Ezekiel 28:18.

This rebellion of Satan would go on for several years before his insurgence in heaven.

The rebellion of Lucifer also caused the earth to be cursed; all on earth would suffer all types of illness and fatal disease; no human or animals would be immune.

The pre-Adamites began worshipping Lucifer, fallen angels, and animals (pantheons); their ways became evil as that of the whole earth, in the spiritual realm and physical realm. The pre-Adamites made figurines, apotropaic[101] amulets (idols) to use with their enchantments. Anthropologists have unearthed such figurines dating back to the Paleolithic Era (Lucifer's reign). It is alleged that women acted as shamans (Upper Paleolithic Era 30 KA). The Venus figurines also depict the people's ethnicity; the Venus of Brassempouy is the Roman goddess of beauty.

This also provides evidence of the evil influences and power of Satan to ensnare these pre-Adamites from GOD to himself; these pre-Adamites knew little of the seductive power of the supernatural realm of evil—only what they were misled to believe by Satan. This figurine is said to depict the *fertility* goddess (sound familiar?), to bring fertility to the land and women.

It is not known how long the earth was operating in this sinful state till GOD served final judgment, *the deluge of Lucifer.* These artifacts reveal the rapidity of rebellion on the earth: the pre-Adamites became quite efficient in their crafts—these figurines are made of stone and clay (pre-innovative), dating back to 32 KA. This also validates the hierarchical, Angelic realm; many types of angels have heads of animals[102] and bodies of men. This figurine showing the head of the lion on a man was found in a cave in Hohlenstien-Stadel. The pre-Adamites' pantheon of gods was induced by Satan (שטן; *satan*) and the fallen angels.

101 Gods of aversion, to ward off evil.

102 Ezekiel 10:8–14.

Satan's "I Wills" Isaiah 14:13–15	God's "I Wills" Ezekiel 28:16–18
I will ascend into heaven;	I will cast thee as profane out of the mountain of God.
I will exalt my Thrones above the stars of God;	I will destroy thee, O covering cherub, from the midst of the stones of fire.
I will sit also upon the mount of the congregation, in the sides of the north;	I will cast thee to the ground.
I will ascend above the heights of the clouds,	I will lay thee before kings, that they may behold thee.
I will be like the Most High.	I will bring thee to ashes upon the earth in the sight of all them that behold thee.

Although the flood of Noah lasted a year and seventeen days, Lucifer's deluge was more a critical condition, like any affixed judgment. There would be a visitation, in which it may have been God Himself in Angelic guise (theophany),[103] or one of His numerous Angels (Jeremiah 4:46), and in which judgment would be executed (Genesis 1:2). During this era Lucifer had plenty of time to turn from his ways but did not! It is not known how long it took Lucifer to influence one-third of the angels and pre-Adamites to rebel against Elohim (אֱלֹהִים), whether it was thousands of years or hundreds.

There was nothing left alive, not even foliage[104]; Elohim's anger was fierce[105] and non-repenting: the earth remained in water and in darkness; the yielding luminosity from the heavens (sun, moon, and stars) ceased to shine upon it. This was different from Noah's flood, in whom He found grace.

103 Visible manifestation of God.

104 Jeremiah 23:24.

105 I beheld, and, lo, the fruitful place was a wilderness, and all the cities thereof were broken down at the presence of the Lord, and by his fierce anger (Jeremiah 4:26).

Speaking of Satan,

> *I know well the method he used. He uses the same method still today in leading deceived humans into disloyalty, rebellion, and self-centered opposition against GOD's government. First, he turns one or two to envy, jealousy and resentment over an imagined injustice—then into disloyalty. Then he uses that one or two, like a rotten apple in a crate, to stir up resentment, feelings of self-pity, disloyalty and rebellion in others next to it until the whole crate is rotten, so Satan proceeds.*
>
> —Herbert W. Armstrong
> *Mystery of the Ages*, p. 66

This present (GENESIS 1:2) state of the earth has been glaciated and thawed (which was repetitive during this era) in preparation for the creation of man (Adam). The earth has been created as far back as 4.6 GA, not only the 6 KA years of man. Further proof that there was a world before is that Satan (שָׂטָן) was already a fallen angel during the rule of Adam on the planet earth (before Adam's fall), which further denotes Adam's *Eden*[106] rather than Lucifer's Eden.[107] In GENESIS 3:1–13 the serpent[108] is an agent of Lucifer, therefore again eliminating all possibility that this is the same Eden (of Lucifer); nevertheless, here is a serpent, not Lucifer himself as in EZEKIEL 28:13-14.

Angels have absolute liberty on other planets in our solar system as they did with the earth in the beginning; the ruler then was Lucifer (Dispensation of Angels), not men; nevertheless, the star and sons of GOD rejoiced at the creation of the earth (Job 38:4–7). EZEKIEL 28:11–17 tells of this anointed cherub who was perfect in all his ways. GOD was no respecter of persons when

106 Genesis 2:8.

107 Ezekiel 28:13.

108 2 Corinthians 11:35.

it came to transgression of His laws[109]; Angels were tested and had a choice to submit to God and remain subservient unto Him. That was so with the majority of the Angels, with the exception of the one-third and Lucifer. As in man's insurgence, God made a special place for those angels who have committed the same sin.[110]

Because of the rebellion of Lucifer and the angels, judgment was eminent. The whole planet earth would become void and submerged in water (Genesis 1:2). No living creatures would survive: not men, vegetation, dinosaurs, marine life, the fowl of the air, animals, nor creeping things.[111] Not only the earth suffered judgment; the whole universe suffered it as well.

This turned men's hearts away from God; men began worshipping idols, many of which were in the images of angels. Not only did rebellion start here but so did false gods and goddesses with similarities to those of Babylon. The rebellion of Lucifer and one-third of the Angels and pre-Adamites caused the earth to be cursed, which was then followed by judgment; a global flood[112] left the earth totally submerged in water and exterminated all life forms.

Illumination from the sun, moon, and stars that ruled the day and night was no longer yielded upon the earth. When the earth was cursed, the mountains trembled and the hills moved, there were no pre-Adamites, and all the birds fled; the place that had once been fruitful had become a wilderness, with the cities broken down at the presence of Y^E^hovah. There was no longer a social system; the cities, in which these men lived in, separated by nation, were no longer.

109 Whosoever committeth sin transgresseth also the law: for sin is the transgression of the law (1 John 3:4, KJV).

110 Then shall he say also unto them on the left hand, Depart from me, ye cursed, into everlasting fire, prepared for the devil and his Angels (Matthew 25:41, KJV).

111 Jeremiah 4:23–26.

112 Who laid the foundations of the earth, that it should not be removed for ever. Thou coveredst it with the deep as with a garment: the waters stood above the mountains (Psalm 104:5–6, KJV). Whereby the world that then was, being overflowed with water, perished (2 Peter 3:6, KJV).

The Floods of LUCIFER *and Noah*

LUCIFER'S DELUGE	SCRIPTURE	NOAH'S DELUGE	SCRIPTURE
PRIDE OF LUCIFER	ISAIAH 14:12–14	FALLEN ANGELS AND DAUGHTERS OF MEN	GENESIS 6:1–7
THE EARTH WAS MADE VOID.	GENESIS 1:2	THE EARTH WAS NOT MADE VOID.	GENESIS 8:22
ILLUMINATIONS FROM THE HEAVENS WITHHELD	GENESIS 1:3	ILLUMINATION FROM THE HEAVENS	GENESIS 8:22
FOLIAGE OBLITERATED	JEREMIAH 4:25	FOLIAGE NOT OBLITERATED	GENESIS 8:11
DELUGE UPHELD	GENESIS 1:2	DELUGE NOT UPHELD	GENESIS 8:11
NO MAN LEFT	GENESIS 1:26–28; JEREMIAH 4:25	4 MEN AND 4 WOMEN SPARED	GENESIS 6:18
DAY AND NIGHT CEASED	GENESIS1:2	DAY AND NIGHT REMAINED	GENESIS 1:5; 8:11–12
NO FOWL	JEREMIAH 4:23–25	FOWL REMAINED	GENESIS 1:22
NO FAVOR FOUND	PSALMS 104:9	NOAH FOUND FAVOR IN THE SIGHT OF THE LORD	GENESIS 6:8

The other of angels who remained devoted to GOD were identified as elect angels[113]. Lucifer and his cohorts positioned themselves as they watched from the second heavens (principalities in the air). **SECOND HEAVENS** contemplated regaining the earth as ELOHIM recreated the earth for man and created man in *His own image*.

Satan's jealousy would continue and become religiously indignant and vindictive over the advances of man, who was visiting other planetary systems, building on what ELOHIM had created and intended, therefore validating his (man's) stewardship over the earth and, increasingly, over the universe. Satan therefore caused divergence between men and GOD as he once had before, as Lucifer the schemer, but with a wider range of associates, which brought into

113 I charge thee before GOD, and the Lord JESUS Christ, and the elect Angels, that thou observe these things without preferring one before another, doing nothing by partiality (1 Timothy 5:21, KJV).

play extraterrestrial life forms with the aid of the fallen Angels from one of the nine levels of the angelic hierarchy. Satan's influences are not only in the earth but also above, even in the universes; I reiterate we cannot be ignorant of Satan's devices or schemes!

It was during the Upper Paleolithic Era (4 KA) that the judgment of GOD was implemented upon the earth and all that dwelt in the earth.

Timeline of the Creation of the Earth to the Creation of Man (Adam), Genesis 1:1–2

EARLY CRETACEOUS II	125 MA–99 MA	
HADEAN EON	4.8 GA	NEWLY CREATED EARTH IS ROCKY; "HADEAN" FROM "HADES," HELL ALGAE
ARCHEAN EON	3.8 GA	
PROTEROZOIC EON	2.5 GA–542 MA	
• PALEOPROTEROZOIC ERA	2.5 GA–1.6 GA	
• MESOPROTEROZOIC ERA	1.6 GA–1.0 GA	
• NEOPROTEROZOIC ERA	1 GA–542 MA	
ARCHEAN EON	3.8 GA	
PHANEROZOIC EON	545 MA	
ACCELERATION OF LIFE-FORMS	600 MA	
CAMBRIAN PERIOD	545 MA	SHELLFISH
FOSSIL FUEL	540 MA	
CAMBRIAN PERIOD	530 MA	RADIATION ACCELERATION OF MULTIFACETED LIFE FORMS ANIMALS; COLONIAL MICROFOSSILS
CAMBRIAN-ORDOVICIAN EXTINCTION (x2)	488 MA–443 MA 440 MA–450 MA	LASTING 36 MA
DEVONIAN EXTINCTION	375 MA–355 MA	
MESOZOIC ERA	251 MA–65 MA	AGE OF THE REPTILES
ARCHOSAUROMORPH (RULING LIZARDS)	300 MA–245 MA	DIAPSID REPTILES: CROCODILES, PTEROSAURS, AND DINOSAURS
PERMIAN-TRIASSIC EXTINCTION	251 MA	
TRIASSIC PERIOD	251 MA–199 MA	
ICHTHYOSAURS (FISH LIZARDS)	245 MA	GIANT MARINE REPTILES
TRIASSIC-JURASSIC EXTINCTION	205 MA	
JURASSIC PERIOD	199 MA–145 MA	TRANSITION
CRETACEOUS PERIOD	145 MA–65 MA	WARM CLIMATE
EARLY CRETACEOUS	146 MA–125 MA	EARLY CRETACEOUS
• CENOMANIAN EPOCH	99 MA	
• TURONIAN EPOCH	93 MA	
• CONIACIAN EPOCH	89 MA	
• SANTONIAN EPOCH	85 MA	
LATE CRETACEOUS	99 MA–83 MA	ALL FORMS OF DINOSAURS; VERTEBRATES, AND INVERTEBRATES; ECHINODERMATA
RESURGENCE OF MARINE LIFE FORMS	100 MA	
CAMBRIAN RADIATION	70 MA	ACCELERATED DIVERSITY OF ANIMALS
K-T EXTINCTION	65 MA	CRETACEOUS-TERTIARY EXTINCTION
PALEOGENE PERIOD	65.5 MA–23 MA	

• Eocene Epoch	55 MA–32 MA	MAMMALS, NEW ANIMAL LIFE FORMS
• Oligocene Epoch	30 MA–23 MA	MAMMALS
• Neogene Epoch	23 MA–2.5 MA	MAMMALS AND BIRDS
Pliocene Epoch	5.3 MA–2.5 MA	
Ardi	4.4 MA	BIPEDAL HOMINIDS
Wooly mammoth	4.8 MA	
Lower Paleolithic Era	2.5 MA–100 KA	
Pleistocene Epoch	2.5 MA–12 KA	
Lucy	2.0 MA	Bipedal hominids
Homo erectus	1.8 MA	Ape (hominids)
Neanderthal	600 KA	Ape (hominids)
pre-Adamites	300 KA–200 KA	orgin Africa (human)
Middle Paleolithic Era	300 KA–30 KA	
Upper Paleolithic Era	50 KA–10 KA	
Cro-Magnon	28 KA	Ape (hominids)
Holocene Epoch	17 KA–10 KA	New Stone Age
Neolithic Era	12 KA–9500 BC	New Stone Age
Younger Dryas Stadial	12.8 KA–11.5 KA	also called the Big Freeze
Mesolitihic Era	11.6 KA	Middle Stone Age
Jericho	10,500 BC–9000 BC	first city
Neolithic Revolution	9000 KA	
Chalcolithic era	4000 BC–3000 BC	Copper Age
Lucifer's flood	4004 BC	
Antediluvian Era	4004 BC–2300 BC	
Adam	4004 BC	
Noah's flood	2348 BC	
Abram and Sarai	2200 BC/1921 BC	
Bronze Age	3200 BC–1200 BC	
Israel enters Egypt	1800 BC–1700 BC	patriarchal structure
Israel leaves Egypt	1491 BC	
Joshua	1400 BC	destruction of Jericho
Iron Age	1200 BC–1000 BC	
Judges	1120 BC	
Saul	1020 BC	monarchy kingdoms
Founding of temple in Jerusalem	1012 BC	
David	1000 BC	
Solomon	965 BC–	
Elijah and Elisha	975 BC	
Destruction of Jerusalem	586 BC	Babylonian Captivity
Birth of Jesus	4 BC	

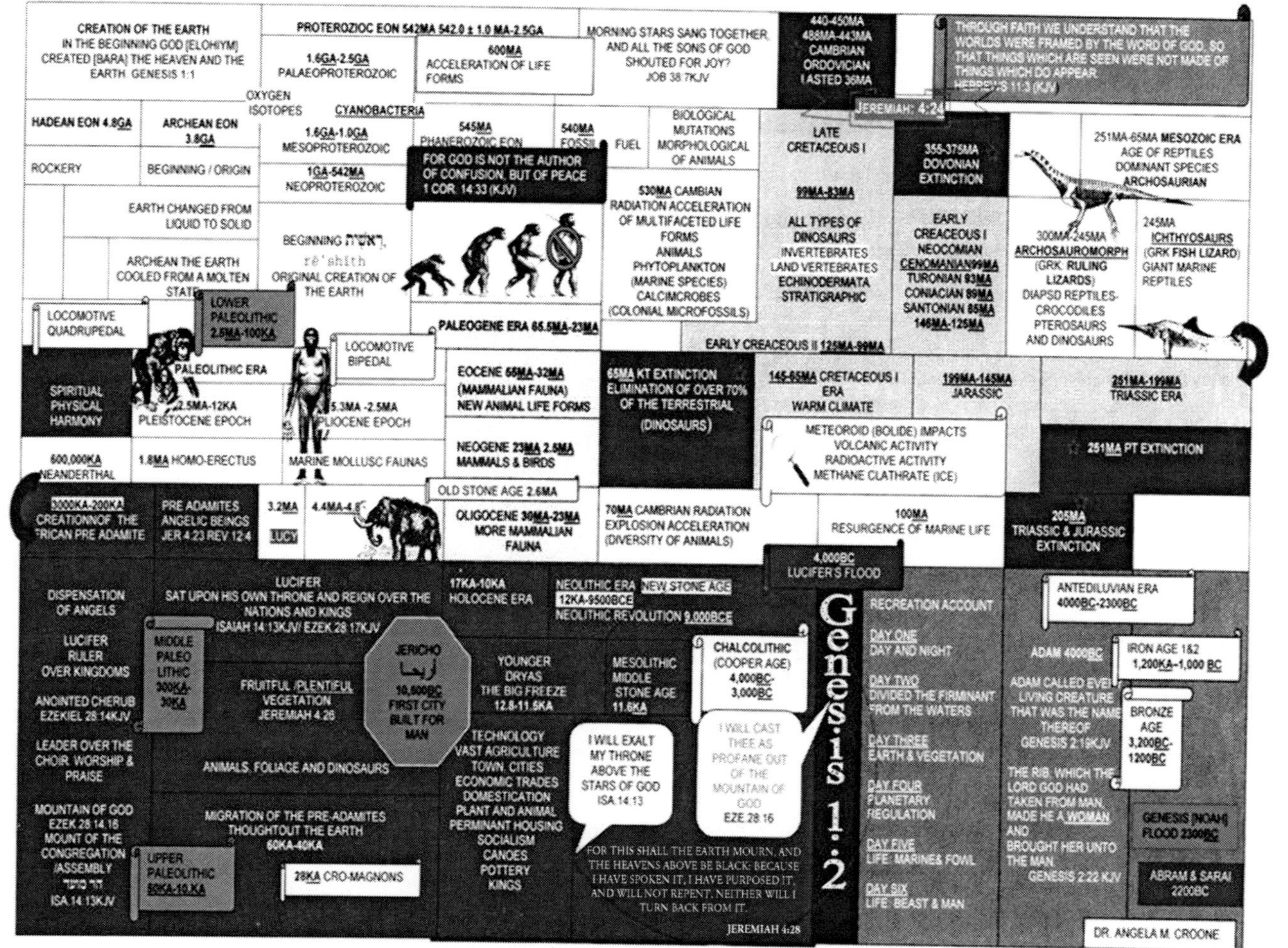

CREATION OF THE EARTH IN THE BEGINNING GOD [ELOHYM] CREATED [BARA] THE HEAVEN AND THE EARTH. GENESIS 1:1
PROTEROZIOC EON 542MA 542.0 ± 1.0 MA-2.5GA
MORNING STARS SANG TOGETHER, AND ALL THE SONS OF GOD SHOUTED FOR JOY? JOB 38:7KJV
440-450MA 488MA-443MA CAMBRIAN ORDOVICIAN LASTED 36MA
THROUGH FAITH WE UNDERSTAND THAT THE WORLDS WERE FRAMED BY THE WORD OF GOD, SO THAT THINGS WHICH ARE SEEN WERE NOT MADE OF THINGS WHICH DO APPEAR. HEBREWS 11:3 (KJV)
1.6GA-2.5GA PALAEOPROTEROZOIC
600MA ACCELERATION OF LIFE FORMS
OXYGEN ISOTOPES
CYANOBACTERIA
JEREMIAH: 4:24
HADEAN EON 4.8GA
ARCHEAN EON 3.8GA
1.6GA-1.0GA MESOPROTEROZOIC
545MA PHANEROZOIC EON
540MA FOSSIL
FUEL
BIOLOGICAL MUTATIONS MORPHOLOGICAL OF ANIMALS
LATE CRETACEOUS I
355-375MA DOVONIAN EXTINCTION
251MA-65MA MESOZOIC ERA AGE OF REPTILES DOMINANT SPECIES ARCHOSAURIAN
ROCKERY
BEGINNING / ORIGIN
1GA-542MA NEOPROTEROZOIC
FOR GOD IS NOT THE AUTHOR OF CONFUSION, BUT OF PEACE 1 COR. 14:33 (KJV)
530MA CAMBIAN RADIATION ACCELERATION OF MULTIFACETED LIFE FORMS ANIMALS PHYTOPLANKTON (MARINE SPECIES) CALCIMCROBES (COLONIAL MICROFOSSILS)
99MA-93MA ALL TYPES OF DINOSAURS INVERTEBRATES LAND VERTEBRATES ECHINODERMATA STRATIGRAPHIC
EARLY CREACEOUS I NEOCOMIAN CENOMANIAN99MA TURONIAN 93MA CONIACIAN 89MA SANTONIAN 85MA 145MA-125MA
300MA-245MA ARCHOSAUROMORPH (GRK. RULING LIZARDS) DIAPSD REPTILES- CROCODILES PTEROSAURS AND DINOSAURS
245MA ICHTHYOSAURS (GRK FISH LIZARD) GIANT MARINE REPTILES
EARTH CHANGED FROM LIQUID TO SOLID
ARCHEAN THE EARTH COOLED FROM A MOLTEN STATE
BEGINNING רֵאשִׁית, rê'shith ORIGINAL CREATION OF THE EARTH
LOCOMOTIVE QUADRUPEDAL
LOWER PALEOLITHIC 2.5MA-100KA
PALEOGENE ERA 65.5MA-23MA
EARLY CREACEOUS II 125MA-99MA
SPIRITUAL PHYSICAL HARMONY
PALEOLITHIC ERA
2.5MA-12KA PLEISTOCENE EPOCH
LOCOMOTIVE BIPEDAL
5.3MA -2.5MA PLIOCENE EPOCH
EOCENE 55MA-32MA (MAMMALIAN FAUNA) NEW ANIMAL LIFE FORMS
65MA KT EXTINCTION ELIMINATION OF OVER 70% OF THE TERRESTRIAL (DINOSAURS)
145-65MA CRETACEOUS I ERA WARM CLIMATE
199MA-145MA JARASSIC
251MA-199MA TRIASSIC ERA
600,000KA NEANDERTHAL
1.8MA HOMO-ERECTUS
MARINE MOLLUSC FAUNAS
NEOGENE 23MA 2.5MA MAMMALS & BIRDS
METEOROID (BOLIDE) IMPACTS VOLCANIC ACTIVITY RADIOACTIVE ACTIVITY METHANE CLATHRATE (ICE)
251MA PT EXTINCTION
OLD STONE AGE 2.6MA
CREATIONOF THE AFRICAN PRE ADAMITE
PRE ADAMITES ANGELIC BEINGS JER 4:23 REV 12:4
3.2MA LUCY
OLIGOCENE 30MA-23MA MORE MAMMALIAN FAUNA
70MA CAMBRIAN RADIATION EXPLOSION ACCELERATION (DIVERSITY OF ANIMALS)
100MA RESURGENCE OF MARINE LIFE
205MA TRIASSIC & JURASSIC EXTINCTION
4,000BC LUCIFER'S FLOOD
DISPENSATION OF ANGELS
LUCIFER RULER OVER KINGDOMS
ANOINTED CHERUB EZEKIEL 28:14KJV
LEADER OVER THE CHOIR, WORSHIP & PRAISE
MOUNTAIN OF GOD EZEK 28:14,16 MOUNT OF THE CONGREGATION /ASSEMBLY הַר מוֹעֵד ISA 14:13KJV
LUCIFER SAT UPON HIS OWN THRONE AND REIGN OVER THE NATIONS AND KINGS ISAIAH 14:13KJV/ EZEK 28:17KJV
MIDDLE PALEO LITHIC 300KA-30KA
FRUITFUL /PLENTIFUL VEGETATION JEREMIAH 4:26
JERICHO أريحا 10,500BC FIRST CITY BUILT FOR MAN
ANIMALS, FOLIAGE AND DINOSAURS
MIGRATION OF THE PRE-ADAMITES THOUGHTOUT THE EARTH 60KA-40KA
UPPER PALEOLITHIC 50KA-10.KA
28KA CRO-MAGNONS
17KA-10KA HOLOCENE ERA
NEOLITHIC ERA NEW STONE AGE 12KA-9500BCE NEOLITHIC REVOLUTION 9,000BCE
YOUNGER DRYAS THE BIG FREEZE 12.8-11.5KA
MESOLITHIC MIDDLE STONE AGE 11.6KA
CHALCOLITHIC (COOPER AGE) 4,000BC-3,000BC
TECHNOLOGY VAST AGRICULTURE TOWN, CITIES ECONOMIC TRADES DOMESTICATION PLANT AND ANIMAL PERMINANT HOUSING SOCIALISM CANOES POTTERY KINGS
I WILL EXALT MY THRONE ABOVE THE STARS OF GOD ISA 14:13
I WILL CAST THEE AS PROFANE OUT OF THE MOUNTAIN OF GOD EZE 28:16
FOR THIS SHALL THE EARTH MOURN, AND THE HEAVENS ABOVE BE BLACK: BECAUSE I HAVE SPOKEN IT, I HAVE PURPOSED IT, AND WILL NOT REPENT, NEITHER WILL I TURN BACK FROM IT.
JEREMIAH 4:28
Genesis 1:2
RECREATION ACCOUNT
DAY ONE DAY AND NIGHT
DAY TWO DIVIDED THE FIRMINANT FROM THE WATERS
DAY THREE EARTH & VEGETATION
DAY FOUR PLANETARY REGULATION
DAY FIVE LIFE MARINE& FOWL
DAY SIX LIFE BEAST & MAN
ANTEDILUVIAN ERA 4000BC-2300BC
ADAM 4000BC
IRON AGE 1&2 1,200KA-1,000 BC
ADAM CALLED EVE LIVING CREATURE THAT WAS THE NAME THEREOF GENESIS 2:19KJV
BRONZE AGE 3,200BC-1200BC
THE RIB, WHICH THE LORD GOD HAD TAKEN FROM MAN, MADE HE A WOMAN AND BROUGHT HER UNTO THE MAN. GENESIS 2:22 KJV
GENESIS [NOAH] FLOOD 2300BC
ABRAM & SARAI 2200BC
DR. ANGELA M. CROONE

Vapor Canopy and Plate Tectonics

Reptiles' growth isn't impeded as they age; the older they get, the larger they become, providing the right commendations and conditions. This also applied to men before Noah's flood, when men lived as long as 969 years (Methuselah). This affirms that the BEHEMOTH (בהמות)[114] and LEVIATHAN (לויתן)[115] did exist before the deluge and some time after in which Noah had placed upon the ark various kinds of terrestrials not limited to dinosaurs and their eggs. Life expectancy was longer during the Antediluvian Era (Noah's flood), after which it would decline.

It is believed that a collapse in the water vapor canopy shortened the life span of man and other terrestrial life forms on the earth. This is the vapor canopy that overlays the earth's crust, protecting life from harmful radiation levels from the sun. Some have quoted the firmament (רקיע; *raqiya,* expanse or space) and the vapor canopy as being one.

Before the flood of Noah, the LORD said, "My spirit shall not always strive with man, for that he also is flesh; yet his days shall be an hundred and twenty years."[116] Here is a clear indication that the LORD shortened the life span of man because of sin, as during the Reign of Lucifer (dispensation of angels GENESIS 1:1). The life span of the pre-Adamites and all other terrestrials was two hundred years or more; this would be a extension of prolonged existence through the era Dispensation of Conscience; GENESIS 3:22–8:14.

114 Job 40:15–24 (KJV).

115 Psalm 74:14 (KJV).

116 GENESIS 6:3 (KJV).

MAN	AGE	MAN	AGE	MAN	AGE	MAN	AGE
ADAM	930	CAINAN	910	ENOCH (T[2])	365	NOAH	950
SETH	912	MAHALALEEL	895	METHUSELAH	969		
ENOS	905	JARED	962	LAMECH	777		

A collapse in the vapor canopy and/or an aggressive break in the tectonic plates above the earth and beneath the earth ocean floors would cause the release of an immense, scorching geyser hundred of miles into the atmosphere. After the deluge of Noah, the falling of the water in the vapor canopy and the successive rain would have produced a cooling effect upon the land, causing acute fluctuation in the earth's temperatures, such as a rapid freeze to 150-PLUS degrees below zero Fahrenheit—an ice age. A whole frozen mammoth has been discovered entombed in a glacier of ice; the contents of the glacier imply that the mammoth dwelt in a more placid atmosphere than the present. The mammoth's stomach contents suggest that the mammal was grazing in late July when it was frozen whole.

The outer layers of the earth are separated into the lithosphere and asthensophere. The differential is based on automatic properties in the procedure to transport heat: the lithosphere being cold and unyielding and the asthensophere being hot and yielding; thus, the asthensophere is collapsible basically through heat produced by radioactive decay—the substance that is decaying is largely the radioactive isotopes of light elements, such as magnesium and aluminum. The two can become alternates of each other at different times based on temperature and force. When there is a transport of heat between the two layers, the lithosphere loses heat by transference, whereas the asthensophere transports heat by transmitting, without heat variation.

The lithosphere is separated into tectonic plates; there are eight major and many minor plates. The eight major plates are North American, South American, African, Eurasian, Australian, Indian, Antarctic, and Pacific; amid the minor plates are the Arabian Plate and the Philippine Sea Plate. These plates are all moving in different directions at different speeds (2 CM–10 CM). Lithosphere plates are overlaid by two crusts—the oceanic and continental (which is substantially thicker than the oceanic crust)—which are carried on the asthensophere. The plates are virtually always moving in one of three ways, creating three categories of plate boundaries: *convergent* (crashing), *divergent* (pulling apart), and *transforming* (sideswiping). Volcanic emissions, mountain forming, and earthquakes can transpire down the plate boundaries; these plates are constantly shifting, so they may converge, transform, or even diverge into one another.

Plate boundaries in different regions are subject to different inter-plate stresses, therefore producing three kinds of earthquakes; these tectonic plate boundaries are extensional and compressional. The continents split away from each other swiftly as columns of water blasted through the surface at an estimated forty-five miles an hour, therefore producing the *hydroplate.* The hydroplate theory explains the origin and receding of the flood. The continents would crash, pull apart, and collapse on top of one another, rising up out of the water, with a force as fierce as that of demolition upon the earth. However, creationist Dr. John Baumgardner created another calamitous plate-tectonic representation: *rapid subduction* of the continents. Baumgardner dismisses the theory of the water vapor canopy, therefore ratifying the idea of plate tectonics.

Convergent boundaries are areas of subduction where one (oceanic) plate moves underneath another (oceanic or continental) plate that descends into the earth's mantle as the plates converge. Subduction occurs when two plates move toward each other on an area in the earth, creating a subduction zone; subduction zones have high rates of volcanism, mountain building, and earthquakes. The process of subduction is a consequence of melting of the mantle, which generates volcanic activity—usually, the lighter rock is forcibly submerged.

The Six-Day Creation and Day of Rest

Genesis 1:6–31

Days	Scriptures		Made and Created in 6 Days
Day 1	*Genesis 1:3* And God said, Let there be light: and there was light. *Genesis 1:4* And God saw the light, that *it was* good: and God divided the light from the darkness.	*Genesis 1:5* And God called the light Day, and the darkness he called Night. And the evening and the morning were the first day.	**Light** God divided the light from darkness. Light, He called day. ***Darkness, He called night.***
Day 2	Genesis 1:6 And God said, Let there be a firmament in the midst of the waters, and let it divide the waters from the waters.	Genesis 1:7 And God called the firmament Heaven. And the evening and the morning were the second day.	**Firmament** God created the firmament, which He called heaven. The firmament was divided, causing waters above heaven (1st) and *waters below* the firmanent.
	Genesis 1:8 And God made the firmament, and divided the waters which *were* under the firmament from the waters which *were* above the firmament: and it was so.		
Day 3	Genesis 1:9 And God said, Let the waters under the heaven be gathered together unto one place, and let the dry *land* appear: and it was so.	Genesis 1:11 And God said, Let the earth bring forth grass, the herb yielding seed, *and* the fruit tree yielding fruit after his kind, whose seed *is* in itself, upon the earth: and it was so.	**Dry Land** God dissipates the water, causing dry land. Land became the earth. The water was gathered in one place called sea. Earth brought forth grass; herbs yielding seed; and trees yielding fruit whose seeds are within themselves and after their kind.
	Genesis 1:10 And God called the dry *land* Earth; and the gathering together of the waters called he Seas: and God saw that *it was* good.	Genesis 1:12 And the earth brought forth grass, *and* herb yielding seed after his kind, and the tree yielding fruit, whose seed *was* in itself, after his kind: and God saw that *it was* good.	
	Genesis 1:13 And the evening and the morning were the third day.		

Day 4			
	Genesis 1:14	**Genesis 1:16**	**Seasons, Days, and Years**
	And God said, Let there be lights in the firmament of the heaven to divide the day from the night; and let them be for signs, and for seasons, and for days, and years:	And God made two great lights: the greater light to rule the day, and the lesser light to rule the night: *he made* the stars also.	Lights in the firmament Light to divide day and night, signs, seasons, days, and years Greater light **Lesser light** Stars Both lights are stored in the firmament. Light upon the earth Light to rule over day Light to rule over night Divide light from darkness
		Genesis 1:17	
		And God set them in the firmament of the heaven to give light upon the earth,	
	Genesis 1:15	**Genesis 1:18**	
	And let them be for lights in the firmament of the heaven to give light upon the earth: and it was so.	And to rule over the day and over the night, and to divide the light from the darkness: and God saw that *it was* good.	
	Genesis 1:19		
	And the evening and the morning were the fourth day		
Day 5			
	Genesis 1:20	**Genesis 1:22**	**Water Life Forms and Fowl**
	And God said, Let the waters bring forth abundantly the moving creature that hath life, and fowl *that* may fly above the earth in the open firmament of heaven.	And God blessed them, saying, Be fruitful, and multiply, and fill the waters in the seas, and let fowl multiply in the earth.	Spoken by God Brought forth from the water An abundance of living creatures: great whales. After their kind, fowl of the air and after their kind, both the creatures and fowls were to be fruitful and multiply.
	Genesis 1:21	**Genesis 1:23**	
	And God created great whales, and every living creature that moveth, which the waters brought forth abundantly, after their kind, and every winged fowl after his kind: and God saw that *it was* good.	And the evening and the morning were the fifth day.	

Day 6			
	Genesis 1:24 And God said, Let the earth bring forth the living creature after his kind, cattle, and creeping thing, and beast of the earth after his kind: and it was so. **Genesis 1:25** And God made the beast of the earth after his kind, and cattle after their kind, and every thing that creepeth upon the earth after his kind: and God saw that *it was* good. **Genesis 1:26** And God said, Let us make man in our image, after our likeness: and let them have dominion over the fish of the sea, and over the fowl of the air, and over the cattle, and over all the earth, and over every creeping thing that creepeth upon the earth. **Genesis 1:27** So God created man in his *own* image, in the image of God created he him; male and female created he them.	**Genesis 1:28** And God blessed them, and God said unto them, Be fruitful, and multiply, and replenish the earth, and subdue it: and have dominion over the fish of the sea, and over the fowl of the air, and over every living thing that moveth upon the earth. **Genesis 1:29** And God said, Behold, I have given you every herb bearing seed, which *is* upon the face of all the earth, and every tree, in the which *is* the fruit of a tree yielding seed; to you it shall be for meat. **Genesis 1:30** And to every beast of the earth, and to every fowl of the air, and to every thing that creepeth upon the earth, wherein *there is* life, *I have given* every green herb for meat: and it was so. **Genesis 1:31** And God saw every thing that He had made, and, behold, *it was* very good. And the evening and the morning were the sixth day.	**All Terrestrial Life forms** Dominion of man Earth to bring forth cattle, creeping things, and beasts, all after their kind Man was made after the image and likeness of the Triune God. Man had dominion over all that God had made. Woman was created for man.
Day 7	Rest		Rest

> BUT, BELOVED, BE NOT IGNORANT OF THIS ONE THING, THAT ONE DAY IS WITH THE LORD AS A THOUSAND YEARS, AND A THOUSAND YEARS AS ONE DAY.[117]
>
> —APOSTLE PAUL

The earth was without light; there was no illumination of any kind. The sun gives an immense light that travels at the rate of 194,188 miles in one second, equivalent to eight minutes, twelve seconds to arrive at Earth. The reduction of light intensity belongs to the moon. In all, light was in full remission (withheld) from the earth because of sin, and judgment had been executed. Light ensures the reproduction of the earth, as it is necessary for all life forms. The sun governs the light during the day over the earth, whereas the moon administrates a lesser light during the night. The earth rotates upon its own axis once in twenty-three hours, fifty-six minutes, and four seconds, therefore receiving illumination from both lights.

ELOHIM (HEBREW אֱלֹהִים) called the light day and the darkness night. This would become Day 1. The word *let* is used with that which has already been manifested; everything that was created in GENESIS 1:1 was already present, manifested in GENESIS 1:2, but in disarray. ELOHIM brought forth order out of chaos. The spirit of GOD would move upon the face of the waters, subsequently converting water into vapor. ELOHIM would have to first restore light, allowing the waters to abate. These lights were not only for day and night but also ruled over seasons (HEBREW מוֹעֲדִים, *moadim*), signs (HEBREW לְאֹתֹת, *leothoth*), and years.

The firmament (GENESIS 1:6) would be spread out like a sea curtain (as in the flood of Satan), an expansion segregating the clouds, the sphere whose composite constitutes an unimaginably infinitesimal number of atoms. The firmaments (HEBREW רָקִעַ, *raqa*) elevated, suspended above the clouds, clinched the planetary eddy. The lighter waters became suspended above, and the heavier were sustained

117 2 Peter 3:8.

beneath, forming an atmospheric curtain between the waters above and beneath: OCEANS, LAKES, SEAS, and RIVERS.

After the lights greater and lesser, ELOHIM called forth vegetation; the earth produced grass, herb-yielding seed, fruit trees, and seed after his kind. A seed elm tree can produce as much as 1,600,000 seeds.

MAN	ADAM	אדם	GENESIS 1:26
LIVING CREATURES	NEPHESH CHAIYAH	נפש חיה	GENESIS 1:24
WILD BEASTS (CARNIVOROUS)	CHAITHO	חיתו	GENESIS 1:24–25
DOMESTICATED TERRESTRIALS (GRAMINIVOROUS)	BEHEMAH	בהמה	GENESIS 1:24–25
CREEPY THINGS, SERPENTS, REPTILES, MICROSCOPIC CREATURES, AND INSECTS	REMES	רמש	GENESIS 1:24–25
GREAT WHALES	HATTANNINIM HAGGEDOLIM	התנינם הגדלים	GENESIS 1:21

ELOHIM called for the water (GENESIS 1:20) to bring forth moving creatures, which hath life, and fowl above the earth and all after his kind. In the water kingdom itself are myriad animalcula[118]; 30,000 of these animalcula can be found in a single drop of water. In each one of these microscopic animals (Hebrew רמש, *remes*) are muscles, bones, nerves, lungs, veins, heart, and arteries. The productiveness of fishes is astounding; one can lay as many as a thousand eggs.

ELOHIM said let the earth bring forth living creatures after his kind, and ELOHIM (GENESIS 1:24–25) made the beast (Hebrew חיתו, *chaitho*) after his kind and cattle (Hebrew בהמה, *behemah*) after their kind and everything that creepth upon the earth after their kind. Adam and Eve were at full maturity, as were all things in the ANIMAL KINGDOM and BOTANICAL KINGDOM, MINERAL KINGDOM, EARTHLY KINGDOM, WATER KINGDOM, TERRESTRIAL KINGDOM, and CELESTIAL KINGDOM. In all seven

118 A microscopic or minute organism, such as an amoeba or paramecium usually considered to be an animal (Dictionary.com).

kingdoms, life was already present. God is life; He is the living God, all that He creates is life. There was great emphasis placed on the seeds after their kind. This was imperative for rapid maturity for man and earth's behalf, for resources for food and shelter.

The scripture below illustrates Adam naming all the animals that Elohim brought before him; still distinguishing man from beast, this also describes the type of intelligence that Adam had. He named each animal specifically; many were named after their very own attributes.

> And out of the ground the Lord God formed every beast of the field and every fowl of the air; and brought them to Adam to see what he would call them and whatsoever Adam called every living creature, that was the name thereof and Adam gave names to all cattle, and to the fowl of the air, and to every beast of the field; but for Adam there was no help meet for him.[119]

In the containment of man (body) is housed the spirit of the living God, His image and likeness; Elohim Himself is not limited by flesh, as is man, whom He created. Man (*Adam,* אדם) is created in the perfection and intelligence of Elohim. Elohim created Adam to rule over earth and all that dwelt in the earth: the animals, elements (earth, wind, fire, and water), and also the universe, in which he also had dominion. All was his; the only person higher than Adam was Elohim. Elohim formed man from the dust of the ground.

After the fall of Satan, the Lord again would restore the earth, for the solitary purpose of man, who was given dominion, in which man would become the successor to and administrator of the earth. The seven-day restoration of the earth would cause the earth to yield its increase unto man.

This same method had also been carried out before Lucifer's reign (dominion). Elohim spoke everything into subsistence: the EARTH, MAN, WOMAN, GREAT WHALES, BEASTS, FOWL, FOLIAGE, and CREEPY THINGS

119 Genesis 2:19–20.

(LOW CREATURES), all after their kind. These creatures did not develop by chance or evolve from a complex life form as advocated by Darwin's natural selection theory.

Nevertheless, we read that ELOHIM specifically identifies *man* and *beast* and how they were created and made after their kind. Man was created (dust of the ground[120]) in the image and likeness of ELOHIM, and the animals (made from waters and earth) were made; a recreation. These were SUPERNATURAL EPISODES from the mouth of ELOHIM. Everything was made after his kind, of its own species, rightly divided in its own sect.

120 Genesis 2:7.

LUCIFER	ADAM
THOU HAST BEEN IN EDEN THE GARDEN OF GOD; EVERY PRECIOUS STONE WAS THY COVERING, THE SARDIUS, TOPAZ, AND THE DIAMOND, THE BERYL, THE ONYX, AND THE JASPER, THE SAPPHIRE, THE EMERALD, AND THE CARBUNCLE, AND GOLD: THE WORKMANSHIP OF THY TABRETS AND OF THY PIPES WAS PREPARED IN THEE IN THE DAY THAT THOU WAST CREATED.[2]	AND THE LORD GOD PLANTED A GARDEN EASTWARD IN EDEN; AND THERE HE PUT THE MAN WHOM HE HAD FORMED.[3]

> THROUGH FAITH WE UNDERSTAND THAT THE WORLDS WERE FRAMED BY THE WORD OF GOD, SO THAT THINGS, WHICH ARE SEEN, WERE NOT MADE OF THINGS, WHICH DO APPEAR.[121]

We read in GENESIS 1:9 how ELOHIM dissipated the waters from earth, causing the *dry land to appear*, which therefore asserts that there was a deluge beforehand. The terrestrial lands and water whereby both percentages are assembled, the dry land drawn out by the WORD OF GOD made once again visible.

When ELOHIM first created the earth (GENESIS), it was invisible until GOD made it visible. The earth had to have been previously made in order for the water to have enclosed it and held it in place, setting a bound till ELOHIM removed it:

> THOU HAST SET A BOUND THAT THEY MAY NOT PASS OVER; THAT THEY TURN NOT AGAIN TO COVER THE EARTH.[122]

In all that GOD created and restored, HE counted it all good (Hebrew טוב, *towb*).

121 Hebrews 11:3.
122 Psalm 104:9.

Adam

AND GOD SAID, *LET US MAKE MAN IN OUR IMAGE, AFTER OUR LIKENESS.*

The ARCHAIC *HOMO SAPIENS* and the PRE-ADAMITES were nothing in comparison to ADAM, in whom GOD had breathed; ADAM was able to name all the animals according to their biological characteristics.

GENESIS 2:7–8 (KJV)

7
AND THE LORD GOD
FORMED MAN OF THE DUST
OF THE GROUND, AND
BREATHED INTO HIS
NOSTRILS THE BREATH OF
LIFE; AND MAN BECAME A
8 **LIVING SOUL.**
AND THE LORD GOD
PLANTED A GARDEN
EASTWARD IN EDEN; AND
THERE HE PUT THE MAN
WHOM HE HAD FORMED.

GENESIS 2:15–16 (KJV)

AND THE LORD GOD TOOK THE MAN, AND PUT HIM INTO THE GARDEN OF EDEN TO **DRESS IT AND TO KEEP IT.** AND THE LORD GOD COMMANDED THE MAN, SAYING, OF EVERY TREE OF THE GARDEN THOU MAYEST FREELY EAT.

ADAM WAS KNOWLEDGABLE ABOUT CULTIVATION AND AGRICULTURE.

GENESIS 2:19–20 (KJV)

1 AND OUT OF THE GROUND
5 **THE LORD GOD FORMED**
EVERY BEAST OF THE FIELD,
1 AND EVERY FOWL OF THE AIR;
6 AND **BROUGHT THEM UNTO**
ADAM TO SEE WHAT HE
WOULD CALL THEM: AND
WHATSOEVER ADAM CALLED
EVERY LIVING CREATURE,
THAT WAS THE NAME
THEREOF. **AND ADAM GAVE**
NAMES TO ALL CATTLE, AND
TO THE FOWL OF THE AIR,
AND TO EVERY BEAST OF THE
FIELD; BUT FOR ADAM THERE
WAS NOT FOUND AN HELP
MEET FOR HIM.

THIS PROVES HOW ARTICLATE AND INTELLIGENT ADAM WAS SHORTLY AFTER BEING FORMED.

EVERYTHING WAS FORMED FROM THE VERY SAME EARTH THAT WAS CREATED IN GENESIS 1:1; THIS IS A RECREATION OF LIFE.

AND OUT OF THE GROUND MADE THE LORD GOD TO GROW EVERY TREE THAT IS PLEASANT TO THE SIGHT, AND GOOD FOR FOOD; THE TREE OF LIFE ALSO IN THE MIDST OF THE GARDEN, AND THE TREE OF KNOWLEDGE OF GOOD AND EVIL.

GENESIS 2:9 (KJV)

The Dominion of Adam

HEAVENS	EARTH	GREAT LIGHT	LESSER LIGHT
LIGHT (MORNING)	DARKNESS (EVENING)	CREATURES WITH LIFE	FOWL OF THE AIR
GRASS	HERBS	CREATURES IN WATER	CATTLE
DAYS	YEARS	CREEPING THINGS	BEASTS[5]

After Elohim had created the vegetation and all life forms, He created man in His image, His likeness. Being created in the image of Elohim, encasing His Spirit, man was able to have dominion over all that Elohim had created, and Elohim brought forth all the animals to Adam that he might name them. Elohim had Adam exercise his authority, and charged him to take dominion over all that He had created. Adam was now steward over all the earth. Man not only had dominion; he would be crowned with honor and glory for this awesome covenant.[123] In this covenant, Adam would be held accountable for how he managed the earth and maintained all that dwelt therein, with the exception that man is a little lower than the Angels.

Adam didn't just have dominion; with that dominion came wealth and ownership, for the earth is rich with all types of precious gemstones and gold.[124] Adam had no need; he was well provided for. He was *wealthy spiritually, physically,* and *mentally,* excluding

123 For thou hast made him a little lower than the angels, and hast crowned him with glory and honour. Thou madest him to have dominion over the works of thy hands; thou hast put all things under his feet (Psalm 8:5–6, KJV).

124 The name of the first is Pison: that is it which compasseth the whole land of Havilah, where there is gold; And the gold of that land is good: there is bdellium and the onyx stone (Genesis 2:11–12, KJV).

a helpmeet, which was brought before him by the Lord shortly after the naming of the animals.

> *"This is now bone of my bones, and flesh of my flesh: she shall be called Woman, because she was taken out of Man."*[125]

The WOMAN (אִשָּׁה, 'ishshāh)[126] was fashioned after man, from whom she was taken. Together, they both were to have dominion, for she was taken from Adam's rib to walk alongside Adam as being one but separate and distinctive. Man and woman were created after the image and likeness of GOD.

The woman was taken out of the man, who is in the image of GOD; therefore, woman also bears the image of GOD. "Male and female created he them, and blessed them, and called their_name Adam in the day when they were created."[127]

Within man is woman; this is biblically sound. If it were not so, the woman would not have been created out of man in which she was fashioned. Nevertheless, the WOMAN is the glory of man and created for man,[128] and out of man (duality[129]).

---

125 Genesis 2:23 (KJV).

126 Typified as type of church; taken out of man.

127 Genesis 5:2 (KJV).

128 For a man indeed ought not to cover his head, forasmuch as he is the image and glory of GOD: but the woman is the glory of the man (1 Corinthians 11:7, KJV).

129 Dualism the quality or state of being dual or of having a dual nature; a view of human beings as constituted of two irreducible elements (as matter and spirit) (Merriam-Webster's *Collegiate Dictionary, Tenth Edition*), Springfield, MA, 1999).

Psalm 8:3	Psalm 8:7
When I consider thy heavens, the work of thy fingers, the moon and the stars, which thou hast ordained;7 Psalm 8:	All sheep and oxen, yea, and the beasts of the field;
Psalm 8:4	**Psalm 8:8**
What is man, that thou art mindful of him? and the son of man, that thou visitest him?	The fowl of the air, and the fish of the sea, and whatsoever passeth through the paths of the seas. The fowl of the air, and the fish of the sea, and whatsoever passeth through the paths of the seas.
Psalm 8:5	**Psalm 8:9**
For thou hast made him a little lower than the angels, and hast crowned him with glory and honour.	O Lord our Lord, how excellent is thy name in all the earth!
Psalm 8:6	
Thou madest him to have dominion over the works of thy hands; thou hast put all things under his feet:	

Elohim created man in His very own image, i.e., *His character*; that he may have dominion to rule over all that Elohim had created upon the earth. Nevertheless, everything else was beneath Adam, and with the Most High Lord over him, as in Lucifer's reign. Humanity surpasses anything else that Elohim has created, for man has a spirit, a likeness endowed by Elohim, rendering any other life form subordinate; it is unambiguously profound that man indeed has dominion.

Man is steward over his life, which is governed by Elohim. Humanity is answerable for the life that is given by Elohim, for in the image of Elohim man was created; for whosoever sheds a man's life, his blood be shed, therefore vindicating capital punishment.[130] Life is hallowed before the Lord; this is something only He can give. Neither does the Lord want us to curse[131] one another, for we are in the similitude of Elohim; rather, He wants us to bless each other. He wants us to live; death was never a part of His purpose for us.

130 Whoso sheddeth man's blood, by man shall his blood be shed: for in the image of God made he man (Genesis 9:6, KJV).

131 Therewith bless we God, even the Father; and therewith curse we men, which are made after the similitude of God (James 3:9, KJV).

His Son even came as the *s*econd Adam, that we might find comfort (rest) in HIM, knowing that if JESUS could emulate Y^EHOVAH and adhere to His commandments, having a submissive spirit and surrender all unto YEHOVAH, humanity can emulate the very same (recapturing the likeness of ELOHIM). For the first Adam brought forth death; the second Adam brought forth life: "*I am come that they might have life, and that they might have it more abundantly.*"[132]

1 CORINTHIANS 15:22	1 CORINTHIANS 15:45	1 TIMOTHY 2:13–14
FOR AS IN ADAM ALL DIE, EVEN SO IN CHRIST SHALL ALL BE MADE ALIVE.	AND SO IT IS WRITTEN, THE FIRST MAN ADAM WAS MADE A LIVING SOUL; THE LAST ADAM WAS MADE A QUICKENING SPIRIT.	FOR ADAM WAS FIRST FORMED, THEN EVE. AND ADAM WAS NOT DECEIVED, BUT THE WOMAN BEING DECEIVED WAS IN THE TRANSGRESSION.

YEHOVAH is immortal, all spirit. In contrast, we must vehemently ensue that of HIS righteousness, for YEHOVAH indisputably is without sin. YEHOVAH is HOLY; it is because of this very quintessence that YEHOVAH places HIS SPIRIT within man, that man may became part of HIM, i.e., HIS likeness. This very same *immortal spirit resides within us*, and when we part from this life, that very same image and likeness of ELOHIM lives on while the mortal man dies, returning unto the ground from which he was formed, and the spiritual man lives on, returning back to ELOHIM!

132 John 10:10 (KJV).

References

AllaboutGod.com. The story of Lucifer

Armstrong, W. Herbert, Mysteries of the Ages 2007.

Balter, M., "Going Deeper into the Grotte Chauvet"; *Science,* 321:904–905; 15 August 2008.

the Bible: The Book That Bridges the Millennia; B.C./B.C.E. Timeline of Biblical & World Events, http://gbgm-umc.org/umw/bible/timebce.stm.

Bibleplaces.com: Jericho.

Biology-Online.

Blood, Dr. Brian, Bear flute, Music History Online: Music before the 16th Century; Lesson 35.

Camfield, Benjamin, A Theological Discourse of Angels. London: H. Brome, 1678.

Charles, R. H., The Book of Jubilees, London: Society for Promoting Christian Knowledge, 1917.

Creationanswers.com, How Accurate Are Carbon-14 and Other Radioactive Dating Methods? Gilbert, AZ: Christian Answers Network, Eden Communications.

Cuozzo, Jack, *Buried Alive,* Master Books Inc., 1998.

Dake, Finis, *Dake's Annotated Reference Bible,* Lawrenceville, GA: Dake Bible Sales, Inc., 1997.

Davidson, Gustav, *A Dictionary of Angels Including Fallen Angels,* New York: Free Press, 1967.

Dionysius the Areopagite, The Mystical Theology and the Celestiel Hierarchies (tr.), Editors of the Shrine of Wisdom. Surrey, England: The Shrine of Wisdom, 1949.

Easton's Bible Dictionary CD.

Entouch.net, The Neanderthalensis Hybrid, http://home.entouch.net/dmd/hybrid.htm.

Ferrar, William John (tr), The Uncanonical Jewish Books, London: Society for Promoting Christian Knowledge, 1918.

Feuerbacher, Bjorn, and Ryan Scranton, Evidence for the Big Bang, The Talk Origins Archive: Exploring the Creation/Evolution Controversy: talkorigin.org.

Geoghegan, Homan, *The Bible for Dummies.* Hoboken, NJ: Wiley.

Ginzberg, Louis, The Legend of the Jews II (7 Vols), Philadelphia: The Jewish Publication Society of America, 1954.

Guisepi, R. A., World History from the Pre-Sumerian Period to the Present, The Origins of Civilizations, The First Towns: Seedbeds of Civilization, International World History Project.

Heywood, Thomas, The Hierarchy of the Blessed Angels. London: Adam Islip, 1635.

Hirst, K. Kris; An Yang; Bronze Capital in China, about.com.

Holman Bible Dictionary, Nashville, TN: Holman Bible Publishers, 1991.

Lubenow, Marvin, Recovery of Neanderthalensis mtDNA: An Evaluation. *TJ* (now *Journal of creation*) 12(1):87--97; April 1998.

Nature holism, www.ecotao.com/holism/hu_neand.htm.

Mellars, Paul, Why Did Modern Human Populations Disperse from Africa ca. 60,000 Years Ago? Proceedings of the National Academy of Science 103: 9381. 2006.

Merriam-Webster's Collegiate Dictionary, Tenth Edition. Springfield, MA: Merriam-Webster, 1999.

Moody, B. Earline and Gene, www.DemonBuster.Com, Deliverance Ministries,

Morris, Craig, Neanderthalensis Taxonomy Reconsidered: (Article);Implications of 3D Primate Models of Intra- and Interspecific Differences. Katerina Harvati, Stephen R, Frost, Kieran P. Mcnulty, American Museum of Natural History, New York, December 5, 2003 (received for review February 27, 2003); pnas.org.

Morton, Glenn R. The Neanderthalensis Hybrid,_entouch.net.

Neubauer, Adolf (ed.), The book of Tobit. Oxford: Clarendon, 1878.

Niewoehner, A. Wesley, Behavioral Inferences from the Skhul/Qafzeh Early Modern Human Hand Remains. University of New Mexico Department of Anthropology, Albuquerque, NM 87131.

Poloymeme.com, Neanderthalensiss Distinct from Us.

Rincon, Paul, Neanderthalensiss 'Enjoyed Broad Menu', BBC News/ Science: Neanderthalensis DNA Secrets Unlocked, Science Reporter, http://news.bbc.co.uk/2/hi/science/nature/7630042.stm

Sharp, Douglas B., The Revolution against Evolution (online book), 1993.

Stern, David H., *Complete Jewish Bible,* Clarkville, MD: Jewish New Testament Publications, 1998.

Strong, James, *The New Strong's Exhaustive Concordance of the Bible.* Nashville, TN: Thomas Nelson Publishers, 1990.

TALMUD (TR) (18 VOLS). LONDON: THE SONCINO PRESS, 1961.

THE BOOK OF THE ANGEL RAZIEL (SEPHER RAZIEL), ALSO TITLED RAZIEL HA-MALACH. CREDITED TO ELEAZER OF WORMS. IN HEBREW: WARSAW, 1881. IN ENGLISH: MS. NO. 3826, SLOANE COLL., BRITISH MUSEUM. AN EDITION PUBLISHED IN AMSTERDAM, 1701.

WWW.BACKYARDNATURE.NET/ECORULES.HTM

WAGNER, C. PETER, TERRITORIAL SPIRITS. WRESTLING WITH DARK ANGELS: TOWARD A DEEPER UNDERSTANDING OF THE SUPERNATURAL FORCES IN SPIRITUAL WARFARE. VENTURA, CA: REGAL BOOKS, 1990.

Glossary

Adaptive selection: The adaptation of a life form to its environment.
Aquaculture: the art of growing fresh water and sea water organisms, such as molluscs, fish, and aquaplants.

Archosaurus (ruling lizard): Dominant of all dinosaurs; a carnivorous Permian reptile; diapsid amniotes, a comparative of the crocodiles, within its clade are non-avian dinosaurs, pterosaurs.

Biface: A two-sided stone tool used for multiple purposes.

Bipedal: Using two feet to walk, jog, and/or run upon hind legs or limbs.

BP: before present.

Brachial: A nerve root above the fifth cervical vertabra that extends above the fifth cervical. It sends signals from the spine to the shoulder, arm, and hand.

Carbon-14: a weighty radioactive isotope of carbon of group number 14 used in dating archeological and geological materials.

Clade: a collective that has one single familial predecessor; acategorization of organisms that consist of fossils and living organisms.

Competitive exclusion principle: the idea that two species in competition for the same resources cannot successfully cohabit if other biological and ecological conditions are constant.

<u>CRURAL</u>: LOCATED BETWEEN THE KNEE AND ANKLE.

<u>CYCLOTHEM</u>: AN ALTERNATING STRATIGRAPHIC SEQUENCE OF MARINE SEDIMENT.

<u>DANSGAARD-OESCHGER EVENT</u>: ABRUPT CLIMATE VARIATION; AS MANY AS TWENTY-FIVE TRANSPIRED DURING THE LAST GLACIAL ERA.

<u>DENDROCHRONOLOGY</u>: A TECHNIQUE TO DATE TREES BASED ON THE TREE RINGS; BASED ON THE STUDY OF THE AUGMENTATION OF TREE RINGS.

<u>DYNAMICS</u>: DEVIATION IN FORCE AND INTENSITY.

<u>EPIPHENOMENON</u>: AN OCCURENCE THAT HAPPENS WITH ANOTHER AND IS THOUGHT TO BE A RESULT OF THE FIRST.

<u>EUKARYOTE:</u> A CELL THAT ENCLOSES ITS COMPOSITES WITHIN A MEMBRANE; IT IS FOUND IN LARGE LIFE FORMS, SUCH AS FOLIAGE, ANIMALS, AND FUNGI.

<u>EXTRATERRESTRIALS</u>: LIFE FORMS THAT EXIST OUTSIDE THE EARTH.

<u>FAUNA</u>: ANIMALS.

<u>GLACIATION</u>: THE PROCESS OF WATER COLLECTING OVER TIME AND PROGRESSING OVER LAND.

<u>GREENHOUSE EFFECT:</u> THE EFFECT THAT HAPPENS WHEN THE EARTH'S SURFACE BECOMES HEATED BY GASES THAT HAVE EMITTED OR ABSORBED INFRARED RADIATION AND BECOME TRAPPED WITHIN THE EARTH'S ATMOSPHERE.

<u>HEMIMETABOLISM</u>: TERRESTIAL INSECTS.

<u>HEMIMETABOLOUS: AQUATIC INSECTS.</u>

<u>HOLOCENE</u> EPOCH: A GEOLOGICAL ERA THAT BEGAN APPROXIMATELY THOUSAND YEARS AGO.

<u>HOMOLOGY</u>: A SIMILARITY IN ATTRIBUTES THAT IS CAUSED BY A LIFE FORM'S GENETICS, I.E., ITS ROOTS (A MUTUAL ANCESTRY).

HYLOBATIDAE (GIBBONS); A FAMILY OF APES.

<u>Igneous rocks</u> (intrusive rocks): Within the crust of the earth, an igneous rock has been cooled down from an intensified heat, such as from a volcanic emission, whereby it has then hardened amid other rocks.

<u>Indices:</u> plural of Index, something that directs or points to a particular condition or fact.

<u>Lithosphere</u>: the earth's crust, i.e., the rocky surface of the earth.

<u>Locomotion</u>: movement from place to place; travel.

<u>Mariculture</u>: a unique division of aquaculture, in which marine organisms are farmed in their natural environments.

<u>Metamorphic rock</u>: a rock that has deviated from its original structure.

<u>Microlith</u>: A miniature blade frequently used in the Paleolithic to amalgamate tools. These blades were constructed from prismatic blades, while using the original peripheral edge to sever. On its own, this blade was useless; it was useful only when placed within a handle, which was often made of wood or bone.

<u>Molluscs</u>: A shellfish belonging to the phylum Mollusca and living in fresh water. There are more than 92,500 identified among these sundry, extinct species (marine phylum).

<u>Monogenism</u>: the belief that all humans have a single origin.

<u>Morphology</u>: the blueprint of shapes and designs, whether external or internal, of organisms.

<u>Natural selection</u>: the theory of a heritable clade that makes it more probable for an organism to survive in a population or in its surroundings to replicate, given a flourishing period of time.

<u>Omnivorous</u>: characterized by eating everything, specifically plants.

PALEOANTHROPOLOGY: COMBINATION OF THE DISCIPLINES OF PALEONTOLOGY AND PHYSICAL ANTHROPOLOGY; THE STUDY OF ARCHAIC HUMANS AND FOSSIL REMIANS.

PETROLOGY: THE STUDY OF ROCKS.

PHYLOGENETICS: THE STUDY OF SIMILARITIES AMID GROUPS OF ORGANISMS.

PLATE TECTONICS: A THEORY TO EXPLAIN THE HUGE LEVELS OF ACTIVITY ON THE EARTH'S SURFACE.

PLEISTOCENE EPOCH: THE GEOLOGIC ERA COVERING THE PERIOD OF THE GLACIATIONS 3 MILLION TO 10,000 YEARS BEFORE THE PRESENT.

PLIOCENE EPOCH: THE GEOLOGIC ERA FROM 5.3 MILLION TO 2.6 MILLION YEARS AGO, THE YOUNGEST TIME SPAN OF THE NEOGENE.

POLYGENISM: THEORY THAT POSTULATES THAT DIVERSE RACES OF HUMANS WERE ORIGINALLY DISTINCTIVE SPECIES THAT WERE LIKELY CREATED SEPARATELY.

POTASSIUM-ARGON DATING: A TYPE OF RADIOMETRIC DATING, THIS DATING TECHNIQUE IS USED IN ARCHEOLOGY AND GEOCHRONOLOGY.

PROGNATHISM: HAVING A PROTRUDING JAW.

PROGRESSIVE CREATIONSIM: THEORY THAT ELOHIM_CREATED NEW FORMS OF LIFE GRADUALLY, OVER A PERIOD OF HUNDREDS OF MILLIONS OF YEARS.

PROKARYOTIC: HAVING NO CELL NUCLEUS OR MEMBRANE.

PROTO HUMANS: PRIMEVAL BEINGS.

QUADRUPEDAL: USING BOTH HANDS AND FEET FOR LOCOMOTION.

RACEMIZATION: PROCEDURE THAT MODIFIES THE APPEARANCE WITHIN A PARTICULAR AMINO ACID, CAUSING VAGUELY A METAMORPHOSIS.

RADIOCARBON DATING: A RADIOMETRIC DATING TECHNIQUE FREQUENTLY USED FOR VERIFYING THE AGES OF CARBONACEOUS MATERIALS (ORGANIC FOSSIL REMAINS) DATING BACK SOME 65,000 YEARS AGO BY MEASURING THE LEVELS OF CARBON-14 IN THE MATERIALS.

Rahab: Also known as a sea (dragon); d[a]emon (Isaiah 51:9), a prostitute who aided the spies of Israel (Joshua 6:23); also known as a planet that Lucifer went to and from before the Lord destroyed this planet, causing asteroids and meteorites to assist in His judgment (majority of the extinction periods) against Lucifer upon the earth.

Sediment: the matter that settles at the bottom of liquid or is transported and deposited by liquid.

Sedimentary rocks: Rocks formed from a collective compound of organic materials and minerals; this procedure occurs on the earth's surface delimited by water.

Sexual dimorphism: diversed methodically in size, shape, and color of male and female within the same genus.

Speciation: the spliting of species; the developmental process wherein a new spieces arises.

Stone Age (2.6 ma–2.5 ma): An epoch dated more than 4 million years ago, when tools and weapons were made of stones (pre-metallurigic). Various types of stones were used to make such tools and weapons among archaic *homo sapiens*.

Taxonomy: classification, an arrangement in a hierarchal formation.

Terrestrial: having to do with the planet earth; land bound.

Theistic evolutionist: belief that Elohim is the creator of the physical universe and all terrestrial and marine life forms and that biological evolution is a natural process within creation.

Unison: an agreement or union; all being of one accord.

Younger Dryas: a geological period of abrupt climate change.

CPSIA information can be obtained at www.ICGtesting.com
231810LV00001B/471/P

9 781426 949289